DEFEAT SELF SABOTAGE RECLAIM TRUE MANHOOD

DEFEAT SELF SABOTAGE RECLAIM TRUE MANHOOD

NICK CHONTOS

This book is presented solely for educational and entertainment purposes. It is the intent of the author to provide general knowledge and helpful information on the subjects discussed to assist readers in their quest for greater understanding and utilization of the ideas, thoughts and principles presented. The advice and strategies contained herein may not be suitable for your situation. While all best efforts have been used in preparing this book, the author makes no representations or warranties of any kind and assumes no liabilities of any kind with respect to the accuracy or completeness of the contents, and specifically disclaims any implied warranties of merchantability or fitness of use for a particular purpose. The author shall not be held liable or responsible to any person or entity with respect to any loss or damage, incidental or consequential, caused or alleged to have been caused, directly or indirectly, by the information contained herein.

For more information: Nickchontos.1978@icloud.com

Book cover and interior design by The Book Cover Whisperer: OpenBookDesign.biz

978-1-7376196-0-4 Paperback
978-1-7376196-1-1 eBook

Printed in the United States of America

FIRST EDITION

www.apexmasculinity.com

Dedicated to every father who, through neglect, indifference, impatience or abuse, broke what should have been the most precious treasure of your life . . . We will now leverage your weakness and change the world.

CONTENTS

A special thanks *for the APEX men whose paths I've been lucky enough to stumble across. Your examples have spoken volumes.*

Pastor David Beatty: *Who built on another's legacy, cause the people needed it.*

Pastor Bruce Burkett: *Whose words of encouragement, during my darkest hour, rang loud and true through the canyons of my heart; "I believe in you."*

Rogelio Gomez: *Loyal. Faithfull friend. My brother.*

INTRODUCTION

Apex |*ey-peks*| (noun): the tip, summit or climax.

Substandard |*suhb-stan-derd*| (adjective): below standard, less than adequate, not measuring to regular standards.

Masculinity |*mas'kye-lin-i-te*| (noun): the quality or condition of being masculine, traditional characteristics of being male.

What does it mean to be a substandard man? Per our definition above, it simply means to consistently perform beneath the established standards of manhood. If I were to ask you, are you an Apex Man or are you substandard, how would you respond? Before you take offense at the question and write me off, feeling as though the question itself is an attack on your character or your integrity as a man, you should know two things. One, I ask myself this question every day. The pain of being substandard, for me, far outweighs the pain of having my feelings hurt at being asked the question. To be given one life to live and to spend that life in the doldrums of mediocrity, never finding true purpose or success, is a transgression of sacred things. Especially when one considers the overwhelming availability of strategies and tools that exist to help men become successful. It's sacrilegious. Regardless of your past mistakes, your traumatic upbringing or the condition that your reputation is currently in, we live in a time never before seen in human history filled with the knowledge to grow and mature as men. The tactics to rebuild and develop our character and the limitless opportunities to excel and succeed are at our fingertips like no other time in the history of the world. There is absolutely no excuse as to why we, as men, cannot become apex. I say that with great empathy to those who were raised in environments that were abusive and destructive. Many of us grew up in living situations that were not conducive to developing the character, habits, mindset, and support system required to hit the ground running into a successful life. Yet therein lies the beauty of our campaign. To go from brokenness to apex achievement is the hero's journey defined. I applaud you for undertaking the quest that lies before you, which brings us to the second thing that you should know. Something in you, proven by the simple fact that you are reading this book, is already operating from a place of honesty and humility as you come to terms with the reality that there's not only room for improvement in certain areas of your life, but you also want to improve and become the best version of yourself. An attitude like this is commendable and certainly unique in the culture that we live in today. In an age where men walk blinded by ignorance to the fact that masculinity as a whole is floundering and the definition of manhood is under constant assault, we need now more than ever for men to understand and operate from the truest and most noble definition of manhood. With firm and resolute determination, we as men must understand and uphold the sacred task of apex masculinity lest it fall by the wayside and be forever lost, leaving the world confused and deficient. The world needs good men. Yet men lay sleeping. Will you rise to the challenge of rejecting the toxic ideologies of manhood and reclaim true, epic, apex masculinity?

This book is a collection of stories from my own life, shared with you for the purpose of inspiring reflection on your own life and the condition that your life is currently in. There are principles that one must adopt and implement in their life in order to achieve and maintain success in any area of life and we will certainly cover them all. Also, all of us are coming into this journey at different stages, at different ages with different upbringings that have developed us to have contrasting worldviews on many issues. The beauty of manhood is no matter if you came from abuse and neglect or if you came from money and a healthy support system, once you decide it's time to grow and mature as a man, the principles are the same for all of us. We all want to be better husbands, we all want to be better fathers, we all want to manage our money better and build wealth. We all want to be healthy, positive, value-adding members of the communities that we're a part of. We all want to be emotionally strong and secure as men and function from a place of emotional health. We all want to build a lasting legacy and go down in history as one who affected life in a distinct and memorable way, rather than one who fizzled into eternity as a continual failure never amounting to much, always on the losing end of whatever challenges life brought our way. It's my hope that this book will be a blessing to you. That it will cause you to make even the most subtle changes to the way you carry yourself as a man. For if we can affect the world around us to even the slightest degree in a positive way, then we are the men who have done the greatest good with the short time that we all have here on this dusty rock we call home.

The principles woven throughout each chapter should cause you to look deep into your own life to determine the current level of presence and effort that you are bringing to the table in that particular area of your life. Like it or not, we as men wear many different hats in life. We have different roles that we must learn how to excel in. Depending on how you were raised will surely determine how well you function and perform in these different roles. The agenda here is not to make carbon copies of myself and sway men to live and think exactly as I do, but rather to provoke men to go deep. To be self-analytical. To understand what their obligations are as men and to embolden them to rise to the challenge of meeting those obligations and become the most elite versions of themselves. My ambition in this is to see men arrive at a place of honesty and humility, two perspectives that are essential in being able to ascertain how superior or inferior one is performing in any particular area of one's life. Pride still goeth before a fall, and for men, our unwillingness to own up to the reality that we're falling down in any specific obligation of manhood is certainly the only reason why we continue to be substandard in that area. For example, maybe you're very proficient at being a dad. You connect well with your kids and take the time to patiently discipline and lovingly affirm their behavior, yet you repeatedly struggle at being able to manage your finances and reconcile a checkbook. Your inability to win in the area of finance is cheating your ability to create and enjoy a greater long-term quality of life for you and your family. Maybe you're a beast at your profession. Displaying a wide variety of work ethics, including timeliness, diligence to detail and productivity. As a result of your determined professionalism on the job, you are climbing the ladder and reaping both the financial and promotional rewards that one would expect of a man who is exhibiting apex performance on the job. Yet you're floundering in your marriage to the point where things are often tense and feel so fragile that the whole thing could shatter without repair at any moment. Being able to honestly pull back and diagnose one's level of performance in every area of life is the first step in developing and maturing in positive ways. Honesty, humility and courage are the essential character traits that actually create the ability to see with clarity the true internal state of oneself. As you and I begin this process of discovery of not only who we are but where we are as men, it is important to remember not to be discouraged with whatever determinations you make about yourself. At this point, you are in an entirely new category of man. You are evolving. Only the most elite and superior men are engaging in this conflict of dismantling the decades' worth of toxic masculinity that has been built up within them and developing epic, apex masculine attributes. This is an exclusive club in so much as not many will make the effort, but those who do will see changes in their character and integrity in ways they would never have imagined could be. They will hit levels of success and fulfillment in their lives that many wish for but only a few ever actually obtain.

I speak from personal experience. There was a time in my life where my accomplishments were as follows: meth addict, alcoholic, porn addict, two-time convict. That's it. That's all I could put on the resume of my life achievements. I had no loyalty, no love, no standards, no character, no integrity. I was a slave to my passions, without restraint or self-discipline. I hated myself. I was confused and couldn't understand why I walked under a constant cloud of failure and defeat. I couldn't understand why I didn't believe in myself and why I always expected to lose. Now more than ever do I understand. As fathers, we must break this cycle of toxic masculinity that is so prevalent in our society today or we will continue to produce broken, toxic men.

As the journey to becoming a better man begins for each of us, there will be an initial excitement. Once we realize that *anyone* can come from *any place* of brokenness and destitution and systematically begin to overcome character flaws, habits, addictions, self-sabotaging mindsets and any number of negative and toxic personality traits, we become energized and zealous for more. When we finally begin to see with our own eyes and accomplish with our own hands, success in business, debt elimination and wealth building, it will become a newfound obsession that will inspire you every day to get up and fight to become a better man. One day you will wake up and notice that all the effort has definitively paid off and your wife is madly in love with the man you have now become. As a result of becoming a strong, grounded, emotionally secure man, she is now able to feel safe, supportive and valuable. This evident stability, not only in your day-to-day choices but in your personality, will cause your wife to reach and display levels of devotion, affection and physical intimacy that you have yet to see in your relationship. Up until now, your indecisiveness, selfishness, and destructive and unpredictable character traits and choices have her constantly on edge and unable to reach that place of cognitive rest that allows her to open up and become fully feminine. In my forty-two years of experience in life, I have come across some very strong and ambitious female personalities. Some women are just naturally geared that way and it's perfectly acceptable, but it isn't typical. Most women want to align under the leadership and vision of their man. The bulk of the frustration in relationships with women in American society today is that, as a result of masculine irresponsibility and declining male leadership in the home, women now have to wear two hats. When we as men take a back seat and become castrated tom cats, showing no initiative to lead and develop our families, manage our money or plan for our family's future, you and I force our wives to begin to assume those roles. So now, not only is your wife managing what would be understood as the more feminine aspects of life, but she is now also forced to take on the more masculine traits that you abandoned or never had to begin with. Your wife will lose respect for you. Women don't often want to share themselves sexually with someone for who they have no respect. It's a domino effect that will undoubtedly trickle its way through every part of your relationship. The Apex Man understands the need to create a safe and stable environment that facilitates the positive and healthy development of the people who he loves and cares for. When you're solid, your wife will become solid.

As well, your children will admire and respect the father that you have become. They will crave your approval and your attention. They will begin to emulate your confident and respectful character. Their increasing levels of self-esteem, self-worth and self-confidence will simply be a by-product of you becoming the most elite version of yourself. When children begin to mirror the less than admirable quality traits of their father, you will most assuredly hear someone recite the old axiom, "the apple doesn't fall far from the tree." That ancient proverb goes both ways. If dad is solid, the kids will be solid. Your children can grow up and do well academically. They can have their emotions in check. They can have a sense of governance and self-control over their physical impulses. They can have a level of self-confidence and healthy ambition that acts as a catalyst to launch them into a successful life. It all starts with you, my friend. As a result of your willingness to do the work of becoming a better man, you will notice that people simply want to be around you as a result of the influence of positive, courageous, affirming leadership qualities that now naturally bleed out from your life. The most important thing to remember is that as you birth this new identity into existence, your old identity will, from time to time, fight hard to regain dominance and control. There are now two people living inside of you. The old man who you are attempting to subdue and eliminate and the new man who you are attempting to awaken and empower. The one you feed will live. They will both scream at you from time to time depending on what your life looks like at the moment. When you're stagnant and not achieving growth toward greatness, the Apex Man will shout encouraging, sometimes brutally honest affirmations at you because he knows you were made for more. When things are difficult and the challenges and goals that you have set for yourself are painful to accomplish and achieve because they take extreme focus and effort, you will hear the whiny, pathetic screams of your old man trying to excuse you from the task at hand because he is substandard. Your newfound passion for personal growth and success as a man doesn't jive with his agenda to be substandard. If, on occasion, the old man gets the better of you, don't be discouraged. Keep on the path. Sometimes it truly is two steps forward and one step back. We measure success not by the step itself but by the distance gained over time. Feed the right man.

APEX
MASCULINITY

PRINCIPLE 1:

THE AWAKENING PRINCIPLE

It was late summer 2003. In a gated courtyard surrounded by 30-foot razor wire, I stood alongside eighty other men. Each of us naked as the day we were born with our clothes tossed unkempt in front of us. One by one being asked by a six-and-a-half-foot-tall, 280-pound cornfed prison guard to lift our junk, squat and cough to validate that we were, in fact, not moving contraband from inside the prison out to the vast, unending landscape of agricultural fields where we would spend the remainder of that day hoeing weeds and picking okra under a blazing hot, dusty, August sky. It was here that I had my first awakening. They would always make us turn and face the prison before leaving the courtyard. This is where the first of eight armed prison guards would ride out on horseback with a .30-06 high-powered hunting rifle. We would not see him again for the rest of the day. Hidden among the sporadic clusters of oak, pecan and mesquite trees somewhere on the compass unbeknown to us was the ever-present, lurking yet unseen reminder that even though we were outside the prison walls, we were anything but free.

As you can imagine, being in an enclosed area with that many exposed, ass-naked men carries with it its own image, its own odor. Unfortunately, these sights, smells and later on in the day the sounds of eighty men marching cadence in military fashion, blazing and tearing through oftentimes chest-high grass, thistle and tumbleweeds, will remain with me indefinitely. Our biggest fear during cadence marching through the vegetation was the snakes. West Texas is notorious for being home to all manner of venomous, slithering reptiles. The procedure was clear: stop marching and yell "SNAKE" as loud as you could. The closest guard would then give one inmate permission to decapitate the slithering antagonist. We were never allowed to run. The warning shots always placed an uneasy feeling on the rest of the day. Looking back, I can understand how distressing that time was for the guards as well. On the rare occasion, they'd get a "runner." Someone who had been sentenced to more time than they could handle. Everyone knew we were miles away from the nearest town. There was nowhere to run to across those flat, open fields. The only reason anyone would dare to make a break for it was because they were looking for a different kind of freedom. Something a bit more permanent. A bit more final. It was never hard to tell when it had happened. The thundering echo of rifle fire across the prairie coupled with an early day in the fields was all the clues anyone needed to know that someone had "laid it down."

In Texas, inmates are rewarded with "work time." By laying waste to fields that we would later plant crops in, we were allowed to shave time off our sentences. Very few prison systems still run this way. Texas seems to believe there's value in making a man labor for his freedom. I enjoyed the fresh air, even though at times, it seemed hot and dry.

I'll never forget standing shoulder to shoulder with eighty other men, hoes outstretched, positioned to start marching through a hundred-yard expanse of weeded terrain. It was my first time down. I was still wet behind the ears, as they say. I told myself that I would just be a millisecond behind everybody else so that I could watch and learn what I was supposed to be doing. That's when this elderly black man standing next to me leaned in and whispered at me to not wrap my thumbs around the handle of the hoe I was holding. "Looky here now, youngster," he said. "Don't wrap ya thumbs around that stick, boy, it's gonna git ya." I nodded my head like I'd heard him but I had no idea what he was talking about. I wished I would have. By the end of the day, I'd never had blisters on my hands like that. This is not what I imagined my life to be.

Life in the clink was reasonably structured and fairly predictable from day to day. Meals were consistently at the same time, sports were persistently on the one working television and it was guaranteed that at least three times a year, the unit was going on lockdown as the Hispanic gangs got bored and decided it was time to start killing each other again. How lost does one truly have to be to cut someone's throat over ten dollars' worth of prison-made, powdered tattoo ink. You sincerely haven't lived until you've experienced the pandemonium-induced adrenaline rush associated with the chaos of being locked in the same overcrowded, inescapable space as twenty-eight other grown men, several of whom are intentionally trying to kill each other. Time slows way down. There's no referee. The brutality and deliberate barbarism continue indefinitely as blood and bodies litter the floor or until tear gas is fired through the door. The tear gas punished all. Without discrimination and without reverence. Again, this is not what I imagined my life to be.

I clearly remember breaking up a fight one afternoon, something that is not really looked on favorably among the most hardened class of convict. I couldn't help myself. There was a pretty intense game of dominoes going on before Pipsqueak (a young white kid with no filter on his mouth and no experience in the joint) popped off and called Beasley (an older black man) a forbidden insult. It happened so fast. Beasley was holding a palmful of dominoes and *WAK*! He kindly smacked Pipsqueak with those bones neatly and direct in his unfiltered, inexperienced mouth. Now most inmates would consider this nothing more than an educational moment for

Pipsqueak and let it be. Something was off this time though. Beasley had been talking funny the last couple of days. Going on about how it wasn't right that they had given him a twenty-five-year sentence and how he'd be an old-ass man when he finally got out. He snapped. Sometimes it took a minute for the reality to set in of what one was really up against. He kept pounding, pounding, pounding. By the time I had got over to them, Beasley had Pipsqueak up against a wall, lying facedown. Pipsqueak's eyes were closed, bleeding. I grabbed Beasley and told him, "If you stop now, bro, you might get away with it. Let him be, no harm, no foul. The guards ain't seen nothin' yet." By this time, someone had pushed the panic button to intercom call the guards. Beasley got a few more kicks in before being cuffed and hauled off to administrative segregation. Pipsqueak picked himself up and stumbled to the infirmary. We never saw either of them again. The icing on the cake for the other twenty-six of us left in B wing unit 3 was when the guard came in to collect all of Pipsqueak's commissary and personal belongings. She was female, brand new and visibly nervous at being in that dorm cell alone with twenty-six hardened criminals. Pipsqueak had a bottom bunk. As she bent down to retrieve his possessions from under his bunk, because of where her pepper spray can was positioned on her utility belt, she somehow inadvertently decompressed the contents of the pepper spray can into her own face and filled our happy li'l frat house with some of the most toxic and noxious perfume I have ever had the misfortune of inhaling. She obviously ran out, leaving a breadcrumb trail of Pipsqueak's belongings behind her. No apology, no amends.

Nothing to remember her by except the aromatic scent of rookie stupidity, burning eyes and a tight cough. Thanks, cupcake. We never saw her again either.

Going back to that day in the okra fields, my awakening day, looking inward, looking upward, looking around at the faces of the men who, like me, had violated to one degree or another Texas state law and had found themselves on the back end of a lifetime of wrong choices, I noticed a common theme—acceptance.

In the faces of these men, men like me with prison sentences fluctuating anywhere from two years up to triple-stacked life sentence convictions, I noticed an almost yawning, consensual indifference to their current situation. Like a quiet, permissible compliance to the present reality that stood before them. These were men who had "given up the ghost," so to speak, of ever hoping to live successful, prosperous and highly rewarding lives. These were broken men, damaged goods. Men who somewhere along their journey had been failed by those responsible for supplying them with the appropriate guidance, training, and loving discipline that would have seen a totally different outcome for them had it been carried out, developed, and enforced. These were men who had finally come to terms with the idea that this was a normal, acceptable life. These were men who had no impulse or desire to see themselves as grounded, successful, value-adding members of the communities in which they used to be a part of. These were men who were resigned to accept our society's cold and unforgiving label of them as outcasts, unregenerate monsters who have no place among the rest of law-abiding society.

My name is Nick Chontos. My Texas Department of Corrections number is 932296. My awakening moment metastasized into action as I began to embark on my second hitch inside those cold, graying, compact, cinderblock walls that serve as a reminder to all who ever gaze upon them that, as long as you and I remain the same, we will always be welcome there. I was, at this point, being flooded with the realization that my addiction to methamphetamines, porn and alcohol coupled with some severely deficient parenting techniques from an emotionally insecure, short-fused, often tyrannical father had created within me a mindset of brokenness and despair. I was a man absent of self-worth, self-image, self-esteem, self-confidence, and self-respect. The pain of growing up in what was perceived as an environment without love or support in a physically, emotionally, verbally and mentally abusive home had caused me to medicate my past with all things destructive. It set into motion a repetitive cycle of sin, shame, regret, repeat that only fueled my desire to "check out" as a man and do whatever it took, legal or otherwise, to fuel an insatiable lust for anything that could take away, even if only for a moment, the pain of a broken past.

How many of the men beside me were just as I? The failed product of addiction, family dysfunction and a lifetime of shameful regrets for decisions made in the moment by men who had become so governed by their fleshly passions. Men who had developed a weakened ability of restraint to stop themselves before ever crossing over the proverbial line to another heartbreaking decision that would ultimately cost them years of their lives.

How many of the men beside me would ever reclaim true manhood, true masculinity and begin the long, arduous journey of personal growth and development that would lead them out of this cycle of pain, suffering and defeat to live a life of real meaning, purpose and success?

The numbers do not lie. The recidivism rates in America are continually on the rise, with 70 percent of all felons being reincarcerated within three years of their release. Statistically speaking, as men, we're not winning. Without true and lasting rehabilitation, without a massive and dynamic shift in perspective that causes these men to radically change the way they see themselves and to change what they believe to be true about themselves, then forever they must remain in the revolving door pattern of incarceration. Until, as they say, the cell is locked and the key is finally thrown away, granting them permanent residency at another failed and broken institution. Sadly, the story usually ends with the prison groundskeeper tossing the last shovelful of loose earth over their lifeless corpse. Leaving nothing for legacy except a mile-long rap sheet, fatherless children who they've sired somewhere along the journey who will often gravitate the same direction, and the heartache of another life that could have looked so much different if the awakening principle had been received and acted on to generate and gain the necessary momentum to take even the most basic and fundamental, actionable steps to begin the process of changing one's life forever for the good.

The amount of courage that it takes for these men to begin this process is monumental. Remember, they are functioning from a place oftentimes completely devoid of self-identity, self-worth, self-image, self-esteem, self-confidence and self-respect. The self-identity crisis is a result of growing up in a living situation devoid of fatherly or positive masculine influence. The foundation of our identities as men stems from the example that is set for us in the home during our youth and adolescence. Without a positive masculine role model in the home, men grow up having no clue who they are. In fact, everything, from how we treat women and how we handle money to our work ethic or lack thereof, simply put, our entire worldview, is molded and shaped by the masculine influences that surround us as we grow into men. Even when the influence is negative, there is still at least some type of transferable identity that lets a man know who he is. Having no sense of self-identity creates only confusion and a feeling of being lost and isolated. This only adds chaos to the situation. An important aspect of self-identity is our levels of self-discipline and self-restraint. When these essential aspects of our character as men are absent or underdeveloped, then we find ourselves easily giving in to the carnal impulses that naturally exist in our flesh. When you couple this self-restraint deficiency with having no real moral compass of what is right or wrong, you will often get men who make choices moment to moment to gratify their flesh, only without any thought for the consequences of their actions. Everything that they seek to do is pleasure-based. Mostly just to offset the constant mental anguish of a broken childhood. Life basically turns into a constant attempt to raise dopamine levels in the brain to create a tangible sense of "feelable" pleasure to take away the heartache associated with feeling lost, abused, neglected, abandoned, and so on. The unfortunate problem with this is that most of the decisions that one makes to create the dopamine rush in their brains to feel better are usually either against the law, harmful to one's self or shameful by society's standards.

For example, the more intense the orgasm, the more dopamine is released. For one simply trying to medicate themselves out of a continual place of emotional despair, sex becomes less about romance and connection and more about eroticism and release. Even if the actions one takes to bring themselves to that place hurt other people or violate the natural, acceptable norms of sexual morality in any given society, it doesn't matter. It's simply a numbers game at this point to heighten the levels of serotonin and dopamine that are being released in the brain during orgasm in order to make the pain of a broken past go away. Sex actually becomes medicinal in the same way one would take Prozac or Zoloft to treat depression. As with any addiction, studies are finally catching up to prove that this pattern of increasing levels of dopamine release through sexual addiction can only be maintained by the addict involving themselves in deeper levels of lewd, perverted, obscene or taboo forms of sexuality. Studies show that men who struggle with sexual addictions are way more likely to have had toxic relationships with their fathers.

This is also why drug and alcohol addictions become so prevalent among these men. The reality that exists for them is too confusing and painful to bear, so they attempt to medicate their pain and alter their reality through illicit drug usage and drunkenness. Again, the problem with this method of coping with the memories of a broken childhood lies in the fact that drugs aren't free or cheap. So, once again, they find themselves committing behaviors that are shameful and illegal in an attempt to acquire the narcotics that will elevate the dopamine and serotonin levels in their brain in order to make it all "go away."

During the hard crashes that follow the sporadic times of sobriety, these men are left with the physical discomfort that coincides with rapidly falling dopamine levels and the regretful memories of shameful things done and the people they have either used or wounded in the process. This cyclical behavior pattern unfortunately accomplishes nothing, except a frantic and worsening desire to escape the reality and the reputation that they are quietly creating for themselves by engaging in more destructive behavior.

Our brains are amoral. The brain doesn't have a moral compass that governs its decision-making process. The human brain only understands living and dying. It associates the emotional feelings of depression, despair and sadness that are created in the mind as dying. Simply from a self-preservation aspect, our brain will almost frantically begin to look for ways to elevate us out of the manic state of depression that we're in and, unfortunately, it doesn't care how we do it. It just wants to live and it sees increased dopamine levels in the brain and body as a way to create "happiness" and live. Obviously, drugs and alcohol accomplish this but it is also achieved through binge eating and pornography. These toxic activities create the highest levels of dopamine rush in the brain, in that a person can immediately begin to feel the change; the most interesting part about this physiological occurrence is that no matter how long a person is clean and sober from any of the above mentioned addictive activities, the brain never forgets the euphoric feelings of pleasure that are created and released during some of these less than reputable activities. I've noticed even in my own life after being sober for many years that when I go through traumatic, hyper-stressful or depressive stages, which happen to all of us now and again, my brain will begin to long for the dopamine release that's created through illicit drug use and sexually immoral activity. I'll start having dreams of banging dope again. I'll start having dreams about illicit, immoral sexual activity. The dreams will usually stay with me in my thought processes throughout the day, pursuing me, tempting me. Like high-end business negotiators, my subconscious and now conscious mind are aggressively at work throughout the day and night trying to sell me on engaging in these activities because again, they have no moral compass to govern right and wrong and they don't often attach future consequences with the actions that they are trying to sell me. They just want to feel better and "live."

Remember, stress and pain release cortisol. Cortisol is your "fight or flight" chemical that your brain releases when there are stressful or dangerous situations on hand. From a natural human/animal perspective, these situations would either be dealt with quickly by either outrunning them or terminating them. In either choice, the stressful situation is usually over within a relatively short span of time, allowing the cortisol levels in the brain to begin to subside and return to a natural state of normality. The problem with stressful situations in our society today lies in the fact that they are not short-lived. The mounting stress of bills, work-related issues, social interactions, debt, marriage, raising kids, mental and physical health-related issues and anything else that we're saddled with today in America can seem to go on and on for extended periods of time.

Stress is supposed to be dealt with rather quickly, again, by either physically destroying it or running from it. Flight or fight. We can't necessarily just run from our mortgages. We can't just destroy a stressful boss at work. We can't just leave and abandon our families when raising kids becomes too stressful. Life is really just an ongoing multiplicity of unresolved conflicts. A basket of issues that constantly need to be managed, addressed, adjusted, and so on. Without the right perspective, one can begin to feel overwhelmed by it all. The need to alleviate the burdens associated with the mounting stress and the increased levels of cortisol being released in the body can often lead one to placate the temptations to medicate.

Compounding the issue of stressful times is the agonizing reality that many of these men could, with minimal effort and ease, handle the reoccurring pressurized seasons of life had they only been trained to do so. That is why it is so paramount that we succeed in growing and maturing as men. We must raise our children in a way that this cyclical pattern is obliterated forever.

There are some in our society who would consider the depth of brokenness in these men to be beyond repair. I say bullshit. I'm living proof that we can be repaired and not only repaired but we can go on to achieve levels of success and fulfillment in life that we never even imagined were possible.

Fast forward seventeen years from my awakening moment. I'm now married fourteen years to the woman of my dreams. I have a quiver full of amazing children who all bring me great joy. Each at their own stages of growth and maturity in their own life. I'm at the financial apex of my career in the oil and gas industry, making more money than 80 percent of most college graduates. It should be noted that I only have an eighth-grade education with a GED. I would be a fool not to attribute my success to a power greater than myself, yet I've also learned over the years that great success has more to do with grit, strategy, hard work, risk and determination than it does with flowering degrees and playing it safe by society's standards. I'm also blessed to have a life coaching business, and a successful podcast. Both designed to help men by not only exposing but breaking the toxic cycles that hinder and oppress them. Empowering them to overcome the toxic self and begin to achieve greater levels of success, fulfillment and influence in their own lives.

We can be repaired. You can be repaired. Your reputation can be rebuilt. It's messy at times but I wouldn't trade it for anything. The tug of war between my old man still trying to live and the new man who now reigns supreme is at times like two massive clouds at different temperatures meeting in the sky with such thundering force that the ground shakes beneath my feet. This is war. The stakes have never been this high. I will either submit to being substandard and yield my life, my treasure, my children and my very legacy to this pathetic bastard, or my Apex Man will burn bright like the furnace of a forging fire and burn away all the dross of toxicity and in the process change my family tree forever. The boats have been burned. There is no retreat. One of me will die here. This is the destiny of man.

I stand before you today an imperfect man. Yet, a man who has methodically endeavored to become the best version of himself, wanting desperately to continue this journey of personal growth and development. Not only so that I can achieve the greatness that I am created to achieve, but so that I can break this destructive cycle of toxic masculinity and familial disorder. All it takes is for one man to dig deep, be honest with himself and be willing to start the process of developing his Apex Man. An entire multigenerational branch of one's family tree can be radically and positively transformed for ensuing ages if one man will make it his life's purpose to end the malignant and baneful character traits and thought processes that have, up until this point, ruined his life and polluted his mind. Maybe it's slightly egotistical on my part, but deep down inside of me is the relentless and unyielding need to prove to the world that I'm not the sum total of all my failures and worst moments in life. Rather, I am an Apex Man. Leading the way, leading a revolution in life of bringing men back from the wasteland ideologies of broken, toxic masculinity where they wander aimlessly, uncertain of who they are, where to go, what is of real value, and how to pursue and achieve those epic dreams and visions of greatness that on occasion, percolate deep within them.

Fumbling through the thistle now for almost two decades,

with what at times seemed like nothing more than a dull machete and an insatiable hunger to grow, learn and succeed, I've blazed a pretty decent trail. I certainly have had my fair share of accounts where I tossed a hand grenade into my own life when things begin to go well, but it taught me something. I became a student of self-sabotage. I'm not a psychologist by any stretch of the imagination, but I oftentimes want to know the "why" behind something. Especially something so profound as to how our mind, and the shape that it's in, can determine the immense levels of success and achievement that one can attain or, to the contrary, create a prison that inexorably strangles the very drive, ambition and faith that it takes to build an amazing life.

If you wandered my path, you'd see great progress, especially considering where I started from. You'd also see many a fork in the road where I veered off, only to hit a landmine before returning to the previous fork and continuing on in the right direction.

An ancient proverb teaches: "A righteous man gets up seven times." That would presuppose, I guess, that he must have had to have fallen seven times prior. Simply put, I've learned a few things on the journey, mostly through falling forward. If you're interested, you may trek with me for a span or two. (These days I blaze a pretty decent trail. With greater efficiency and much more joy.) However, you must know that although your path to personal growth, maturity and unbelievable success may have similarities to mine, ultimately, your success trail must and can only be blazed by you. The purpose of walking with me a span or two is simply to tease out some tactics and strategies that you can implement in your own life. Tactics that will empower you and save you time on your journey of becoming the best version of yourself. I would ask only that you pay close attention, take notes and apply what you learn with enthusiastic energy and sincere diligence. Give yourself lots of grace (you're going to need it). There will be days that you get your ever-loving ass kicked. The old man dies hard and life throws you curveballs from time to time. Don't quit. Be willing to do the hard work. Be optimistic about the process of growing as a man. Function from a place of gratitude no matter what your current, starting point circumstances look like. Commit now, in the beginning, to go the distance. To being long-haul-minded. As you progress, you're going to learn how to be proactive in planning your future. In addition to growing daily as a man, you're going to learn how to simultaneously put into motion some key pieces on this chessboard of your life that will pay big dividends in your future. We no longer live moment to moment, pleasure to pleasure. Long gone are the days of living like a racoon, going from one neighborhood trashcan to the next, simply scrounging for the next meal and quietly hoping that there won't be a loose dog to run us off. This is a commitment to yourself. Honor yourself. Value yourself and your potential. You have something unique to contribute to the world. At the same time, the world has abundant wealth and a treasure trove of amazing life experiences to offer and share with you in return.

Remember, there was a time in my life where I lived under a bridge in El Paso, Texas. Nothing to my name except the clothes on my back, a dull syringe and some warrants for my arrest.

Seventeen years later ...

My marriage has never been better ...

My kids are emotionally healthy and love their dad immeasurably ...

I have a fulfilling career that supplies the needs ...

My wife and I together do six figures annually ...

We attend a great church ...

We have solid, dependable vehicles ...

We positively influence people and the world around us ...

Yup. Still blows me away to even think about it. God has been faithfully good to me. It's been an uphill climb for sure though. From the moment I walked out of that prison, I've been climbing. From scratch, learning how to be a better husband, a better father, manage a home, manage my finances, stay sober, hold a job, deal with stress and any number of other life lessons that men need to know in order to excel in life. My willingness to not plateau and say, "It's good enough, I'm good enough," is certainly why I continue to consistently win at increasingly greater levels today. My willingness to not quit after any number of catastrophic failures in behavior or epic blowouts in character is why I'm still moving forward as a man, and believe me there have been many of them. That's why we must give ourselves grace for the journey. Grace is simply "room to grow." Remember ... It also helps to have a good healthy dose of DILIGAF concerning what other people think. (I'll let you look it up.) I've learned over the years that the most judg*mental* people in life are the ones who actually gave up climbing a long time ago. They are the ones who never realized their potential, who never achieved their dreams. They are the ones who expend themselves whispering your faults among each other, exhausting energy on verbally reporting the moment-by-moment headlines of tragedy from the news story of your life, yet never giving single celebratory praise to the achievements that you've worked so hard to acquire. That's OK. We will keep building the epic biography of our life story, and with each successful summit we arrive at on our journey upward, we will naturally create a perpetual distance between ourselves and those who have chosen to embrace the permanent failure of idle stagnation. I can't even see some of those people anymore. The distance I've achieved is too great. Their opinions and criticisms have been minimized and made irrelevant by their mediocre existences. In my kindness though, I shall leave a trail of breadcrumbs ... Just in case.

As we wind down this chapter, I'd like to leave some specific takeaways for your reflection and some actionable steps for you to implement in your life today.

1. The awakening moment happens when we realize that the pain of being substandard hurts more and far outweighs the pain that will be required to make the necessary changes to become apex. The hidden danger here is that we become inoculated to pain. We begin to build a greater threshold of tolerance to the perpetual negative outcomes that substandard living and toxic decision-making create

for us. To the point that things that would have been a red flag for change to most successful people for us are just normal. Being the stubborn mules that we are and simply not being aware that our lives shouldn't have to be filled with perpetual bottom-shelf living, we continue to embrace with comfort and ease the crippling effects of septic choices. Are you not tired of this shit, bro? Seriously, are you not tired of waking up every day struggling with the same addictions, the same paycheck-to-paycheck poverty, the same struggles in your family, the same stagnation in your marriage? Is there nothing in you that even remotely believes that you're capable of doing the hard work of writing out your current hardships and challenges and learning some basic tactics and strategies for surmounting and conquering those challenges? You don't have to fix it all at once, brother; just sit down and write a list of what sucks in your life and then write another list of your dreams and ambitions and take some basic steps to move away from what sucks toward what seems like it will give you greater fulfillment and joy. I promise you as you begin to grow as a man, you'll start loving the process of growing as much as you'll love systematically achieving those epic goals that you've set for yourself. As a side note to this process, it should be noted that those of us who had more judgmental father figures in our adolescence will often be the most judgmental of our own growth. Don't be your worst enemy. Praise the little accomplishments as you go. Defeatism can cause stagnation. The heart issues are more important than the flesh issues. Obviously, yes, you should quit smoking but would you not agree that your wife and children would rather have a kind-hearted, compassionate, self-controlled father who's trying to quit smoking as opposed to a habit-free, heart-healthy asshole who treats people like garbage and has no control of his temper or damaging speech patterns? Make sense? Remember, most of the men have given up. It's really just you and me right now, brodie. Evolving. Becoming. Like an ugly little caterpillar, having spun a cocoon of personal growth and development, we will soon be taking flight daily, being the most elite versions of ourselves.

2. The awakening moment happens when we realize that *anyone* can come from *any place* of destitution or failure in life and go on to achieve epic and monumental success, fulfillment and joy in life. I don't care if you were abused, abandoned or neglected. I feel your pain, brother. I come from deep wounds too, but we have to keep going. You have to learn to leverage your wounds and your broken past to create a more positive and productive future. I'm leveraging the wounds of an asshole father to make me the most kind, supportive and loving father I know. So many people just like you and me have come from abusive childhoods, broken marriages, drugs, alcohol and porn addictions to go on and become addiction counselors, business owners, pastors, loving and highly influential fathers, great husbands and even millionaires. You must begin to believe in yourself. There's nothing that separates you and me. I put my pants on one leg at a time, just like

you. I just made the commitment long ago to never stop growing. I made the commitment to create and accomplish little challenges in my life so that I could gain a growing track record of successes to help stimulate my self-confidence. I just eliminated all the toxic people in my life. When I have a setback in life, I don't hear my father's voice telling me I'm a worthless piece of shit anymore. I now hear my own voice, telling me that falling forward is a requirement to learning how to excel in life. I give myself grace for the moments of weakness. You can do this, bro. I know you can. I believe in you.

3. The awakening moment happens when we realize that even though the process of acquiring broken, toxic mindsets or addictions and underdeveloped self-discipline over the course of our youth and adolescence may not entirely be our fault, it is, however, now our responsibility to crucify them and succeed. We get nowhere when we defer and shift blame to another person, event or circumstance. We understand that parents are responsible for training and developing their children to be successful. If that principle wasn't in play for you growing up, guess what? Welcome to the club. My mother was sixteen when she had me. Her mother was a full-blown high-functioning alcoholic by then. How far back up the family tree are you going to go looking for the culprit to pin several generations of brokenness on? If you did find them, chances are they're already dead. You, however, are still alive. Still able to reform yourself and change the course of history. For

the good. Forever. Do you not yet realize the implications of what's at stake here? Brother, please think long term. As it stands now, the future is not yet determined. The future will happily create for you a life of abundance, joy and opportunities for wealth, love and success. It will also happily create for you a continuation of what you already have. Poverty, defeatism, addictions and emptiness. The future doesn't care what it creates for you. Like a happy little robot, it watches your choices, habits and decisions that you make today and assumes that because you're making those toxic choices, then you must enjoy the result of those behaviors and choices so it creates the fallout or outcome of those choices for you to enjoy.

But you don't enjoy them anymore. Do you? The pain of being substandard is now outweighing what your mind thinks the pain levels will be to begin the process of change. The pain of being substandard is to the point where you now no longer care who's responsible for ruining you as a child and you just want to heal and move on. No one is asking you to forget the wounds. In fact, you should harness those memories and use them as fuel to launch you into a greater determination to succeed. I just don't want to see you get stuck in a place of blame-shifting. It's easy to justify laziness and lethargy at that point. Everything we do is always somebody else's fault; therefore, we need not take seriously the priority of change. When we focus on blame deferment, that means we're not focused on strategies for change. We're losing ground at that point. It's better for us as men if we simply take extreme ownership of our problems, habits and character traits so that we can put laser focus on healing, rebuilding and developing our inner man.

4. The awakening moment happens when we realize that entertaining bitterness toward those responsible for any of the psychological trauma or harm that we experienced as a child will be a stumbling block to our healing and growth. It can be likened to the idea of you drinking poison, hoping that they die. That, my friend, is insanity. We have our own work cut out for us in rebuilding our lives. It's a daunting and serious task. We cannot defer any energy to bitterness or hatred toward others. We will deal with those people later. We must first heal, then get grounded and solid. This goes hand in hand with the last point. We may not be entirely responsible for the inception of these problems, but they are now ours to deal with. The dirty little secret, brother, is that no one really cares. People might say that they're sorry for your troubled past. Be guaranteed of this though; no one is going to lose any sleep over whether or not you change or stay the same. No one is wringing their hands in distress or dismay at the thought of you staying broken, traumatized or substandard. No one is lamenting in anguish or regret at your current plight of suffering and hardship. The cold reality is, they are too consumed with themselves and their own brokenness. They have nothing to offer you by way of redemption. They have nothing left to give. You stand alone. On the battlefield of the rest of your life. One enemy between you and complete victory.

Yourself. Behind him lay all the wealth and treasure of an immense kingdom. All of it belongs to you. Pillaged and plundered from you during a time when your kingdom was weak and frail. During a time when your kingdom was under attack from within. No longer. Self-sabotage and self-loathing have been exposed for the traitors that they are. Their guilty verdict rang loud and true from the halls of self-awareness. Judged and sentenced, their lifeless corpses now sway on the gallows of determination as you march toward the boundary lines of what remains of your life to initiate your relentless campaign to seize and reclaim everything that is yours and so much more. Again, one of you will die here.

5. The awakening moment happens when we understand that real personal growth and success are truly measured by the distance gained over time. There may be seasons on the journey where it seems as though we're taking two steps forward and one step back. For many of us, having a solid father figure or mentor in our youth to train and teach us how to be successful and self-disciplined just wasn't an option. For those of us trying to learn and become a solid, grounded and self-mastered man, we need to grade ourselves on the learning curve. Quite honestly, if you think about it, in this particular arena, you and I wear two hats. We are simultaneously the student and the teacher. You are now overseeing the educational growth and development of yourself. You'll have to, mostly by trial and error, figure out what works and what doesn't. You'll have to figure out

what empowers you and what hinders you. Your triggers for negative thinking and self-sabotaging behavior often lie one layer back from conscious perception. This means that the majority of the world walks blindly in unawareness of even why they continue to be their own worst enemies. It took me almost fifteen years to realize that rejection was a trigger for me. I honestly never considered myself to be one who even remotely cares what others may think or say about me. Not so. There was a time, not so long ago, where the thought of someone second-guessing my ability to accomplish a task was hurtful. There was a time in my past where if I knew that someone didn't want me around, it made me feel unaccepted. Rejected. Knowing now, that all those negative feelings and emotions trace back to my father and even at times my mother and the way they treated or spoke to me allows me to not internalize them so much today. The point is, you have much to learn about yourself. As you go, there may not be anyone there to point out the obvious. You have to be self-analytical. You and you alone will determine if this process of growth and maturity is a mere hobby or an urgent project. You will set the pace. You will provide the course and curriculum of study. You will measure and grade the rate of growth and success. As well, you must follow and keep the pace you set for yourself. You must vigorously and thoroughly attend the course of study. You must be honest with yourself concerning the outcomes and the level of growth that you see, adjusting the course as necessary to keep the best momentum and gain the most dividends. What books on personal growth and development are you reading? (This one, dumbass. Nice rebuttal.) What's your next book? What did you learn? How are you implementing what you're learning from that book on finance? Fatherhood? Sobriety? Marriage? What podcasts are you listening to? (Apex Masculinity, of course. Oh yea, right. Nice choice.) There are so many *free* mentors out there waiting, wanting to influence your life in a positive way. The podcast world is filled with amazing personalities who help teach, train and inspire their audience to grow and succeed in any number of different areas. My personal favorites include Andrew Ferebee with Knowledge For Men, Rewire with Ryan Stewman, Tony Robbins, and Dave Ramsey, just to name a few. The knowledge and the wisdom that's passed down, if you'll be an avid consumer of it, gets embedded into your psyche. Like little seeds of wisdom and truth, they will, if nurtured right, always produce a crop of growth toward success. The point is, my friend, you need to make your healing and growth a serious project. Figure out what works for you. It may be books or podcasts on personal growth and development. It may be NA or AA meetings. It may be seeing a therapist once a month or attending a local house of worship where you can get some counsel or just simply be around other folks who are pursuing a steadier path in life. Figure out what works for you and like Nike says, Just Do It. For me, it's a healthy combination of all of the previous suggestions.

Circling back to my original point, just remember it's a process. Give yourself room to grow. Going forward, I want you to love yourself. For some of you, you are hearing that for the first time ever. Yes, that's right, I said love yourself. Value yourself. For many of us, whether intentionally or not, by the words and actions (or lack thereof) of those around us, we were conditioned to believe that we were undeserving of love and support. That type of demeaning and disparaging thinking gets anchored deep into the psyche of a man and produces only self-loathing and extreme levels of uncertainty in even the most mundane and simple choices and tasks. If we're not careful, this line of thinking can create faulty comparison syndrome where we incorrectly assume that everyone else in life is doing well, doesn't have any flaws and therefore is deserving of love and respect. We know our own selves all too well. Every dark corner inside, every dirty deed ever done. If we're not careful, we can incorrectly assume that others have it all together and because we don't, they obviously deserve love and respect and we do not. You'd be amused and amazed to know that everyone has dark corners in their life. Everyone has engaged in something immoral or reproachable at some point in their life. We're all human. All of us are prone to moments of weakness and frailty. It's all about perspective.

6. The awakening moment happens when we understand that personal growth requires us to be brutally honest with ourselves. As we proceed, we cannot make excuses as to why we cannot grow. As it relates to honesty, our own pride will be our biggest enemy. Especially if we're

the type of person who struggles with how people perceive us. We all want to paint ourselves in the best light in every situation. Self-deprecation is not a natural character trait for many of us. No one is asking you to paint signs and stick them in your front yard advertising to the world that you're struggling with your finances, or that your marriage is falling apart. No one is asking you to pass out flyers informing the neighborhood of your porn addiction or your apparent inability to get your weight under control and live healthy. I could care less if anyone else ever realizes how difficult things have been for you. In fact, I hope they don't. I simply want you to notice and not run from the reality that there's work to be done. I want you to be able to truthfully ascertain your current situation in every area of manhood. With all the different hats that men wear in life, it's essential that we be able to recognize our shortcomings. Unless we are convinced of the seriousness of the situation and willing to own it, we will never begin the process of change. We must commit to the hard work of rebuilding the rest of our lives. In addition to becoming honest, we must also commit to being consistent. For the moment we become idle in this task, we will, by default, gravitate back toward the old man. Usually at a more rapid pace than when we pulled away. Stay focused; inconsistency breeds failure. The reason for this is that you eventually just get tired of trying. Every time you start and quit, you build a track record of inconsistency and defeat. This repetitive cycle of surrender begins to tear down your courage and the self-esteem required to go the distance. There will be seasons where you stumble more. Seasons where it seems as though everything that can go wrong does go wrong. It's good to be mindful of this truth; life gives you nothing good without effort and cost. You need to see those tougher times as the seasons where you will end up growing the most. Growing through falling forward. Remember, you are the grand architect of this construction project of rebuilding your life for the rest of your life. You are the director of the movie script of your own life story. You are the main character in this film. You determine how this movie develops, and most importantly, how it ends. You need to start considering how you can affect life rather than constantly being affected by life. It's a complete paradigm shift in thinking.

7. Lastly, the awakening moment happens when we understand that comparison syndrome is an unhealthy mindset that will breed stagnation and failure in our journey of becoming the best version of ourselves. It's really easy to fall into the trap of comparing our lives to the worst people that we know to make ourselves look better than we really do. We all have an alcoholic uncle who's been married three times. We all have a brother-in-law who's been to prison twice and can't hold a job for more than a month. If you continually contrast your life with the worst person you know to make yourself feel better about how you're operating as a man, then you're already binding the rope about your hands and placing your neck within the noose. Everyone is acquainted with someone whose life

is an obvious and continual train wreck, but you cannot let their botched, inadequate life be the scales against which you weigh your own life. For example, you may be doing much better than Uncle Tony by comparison in that you have a job, but that's not really an accurate system of measurement for you because Uncle Tony is self-employed selling heroin in between his quarterly visits to county jail. The fact that you have a job is commendable for sure, but is it the same job that you've had for the last ten years where you make minimum wage? A dead-end job with no room for advancement where you are underpaid, underappreciated, unfulfilled and miserable? Comparing yourself to someone who's broke all the time in order to make yourself appear financially put together may be the current psychological game you play with yourself, but it's a false consolation. You may have steady paychecks coming in week to week, but your chicken scratch wages combined with your inability to manage that meager fare keeps you just as impoverished and stuck as the next guy. Seriously though, how many American men across all ethnic lines live paycheck to paycheck, bottle to bottle, dope bag to dope bag, relationship to relationship, child support payment to child support payment with their credit cards maxed out in a continual place of stuck. The only highlight of the year being income tax season so we can get a couple of grand back from Uncle Sam to catch us up or keep us afloat for a few months until the next substandard decision. If you just kept making the minimum payments on your credit cards, how many years would it take for you to pay them off? That same amount of money that you waste in interest payments "discovering the possibilities" if invested over the same amount of time in a 401(k) or a growth stock mutual fund would change your life in ways you can't begin to imagine. Please don't see me coming off as self-righteous. I remember having four credit cards, all maxed out at one time. I too fell prey to the temptation to accept overpriced money. I remember it like it was yesterday. I had been out of prison and working for about six months before receiving credit card offers in the mail. It was a first for me. I felt as though the powers that be had decided that I was trustworthy and reliable. The reality is, they were really hoping that I'd be gullible and undisciplined. Which I was. In every way. I also remember getting that first minimum wage job after getting out of prison. I worked in a mulch factory running a machine that shredded newspaper and mixed it up with aspen wood shavings for people to mulch into their gardens and flower beds. It felt so awesome to be gainfully employed. The pride I felt going to work every day was amazing. It boosted my self-confidence and provided a sense of purpose for my new life on the outside. Understand me when I say that work is good for men. I don't seek to minimize the accomplishment of being employed. It's an honorable achievement. If you're working at an entry-level job right now, good for you. Many men have yet even to man up and get themselves a job at all. What I really want for you though, my brother, is to have some drive and ambition to take yourself up the financial ladder so that you can systematically increase your wages and the quality of your life for not only yourself but also for the people who you claim to love and care for.

I remember sitting in the prison cafeteria one afternoon with about fifty other men who had chosen to go hear a prison "volunteer" speak on life change. He was a middle-aged Hispanic man named Carlos who had gone to prison in his early twenties. His backstory was much like ours. No father, poverty, drugs, booze, immorality, no self-discipline or self-restraint. He had gotten involved with gangs early on like most of us had, simply to have support and validation. While in prison, he dug deep within himself and against all odds, he began the courageous, lifelong process of turning his life around. He started distancing himself from toxic people, he got his GED diploma and most importantly, he started reading. After his release, because of his record and his lack of work experience, he struggled to find work. He finally ended up getting a job through a prison reform program that allowed him to work forty hours a week picking up trash alongside the highway on the outskirts of his hometown in Dallas, Texas. It was minimum wage for one year. He showed up faithfully every day, was early and never missed a day. He had a grateful attitude and did his job better than everyone else. The scope of work from day to day was unchanging. Fill up as many bags as you could with trash off the side of the freeway, tie the bags off when full and leave them on the shoulder of the road for someone else to come by and pick them up. As you can imagine, a lot of his fellow employees were guys in an identical situation as he. However, although they may have been in a similar life situation, they were in no way similar in the same mental situation. Most of them were there for a paycheck or two so that they could score a sizable dope sack and start hustling again. Not Carlos. He was committed to himself. He was operating with a different mindset. It's obviously not where he wanted to spend the rest of his life, but it kept him employed and he waited patiently for his break. When it was thirty-five degrees out, he was there. When it was ninety degrees out with 100 percent humidity, he was there. He watched at least sixty men come and go that first year. They'd get a paycheck and fall off the wagon. He could pick them out after a while. The ones who would be there for a week. It was the way they carried themselves, the way they spoke. As men, we're constantly giving off cues and indicators as to where we're at psychologically. He could almost time their disappearance to the day. The first year was tough. Not the work, mind you; that was the easy part. The difficult part was staying the course while he rebuilt his life. He had to get a bank account, save his money and get an apartment so he could move himself away from the drama and temptations that existed at the halfway house. He had to turn his utilities on, cook and prep his own meals and do his own laundry. Up to this point, all of these things had been done for him in prison. He had to get a driver's license and ultimately save up for his first car. He learned how to be consistent in all areas of his life. One morning the boss asked him to jump in the company truck and go pick up all the prefilled bags off the side of the highway. He had already gotten his license so there wasn't any reason why he couldn't. He got everything picked up timely and dropped all the garbage bags off at the landfill by four thirty before returning to the yard. The following morning he was informed that the guy who had been doing that job had relapsed and violated his parole. He would now be the guy who picked up the trash bags going forward. Something that might seem trivial for you and me, but for him it was an honor. He had officially moved up the ladder. He would no longer be picking up trash off the side of the road. He landed himself a small raise. He could spend part of the time on his feet loading bags into the truck and then get himself a good sit down break on his drive to the dump. Back and forth, round and round. Driving around the Dallas/Fort Worth area picking up all the bags from all the different work crews that were scattered out in multiple locations across the region. All his hard work and dependability had paid off. He started meeting people at different levels within the company. Making connections. Building relationships. The fact that people were beginning to trust him though was the most encouraging aspect of his career. He had responsibility of a company vehicle, and a fuel card. No one was standing over him anymore, making sure that he was honest. He honored their trust in him and continued to work hard and rebuild his reputation. After a short season doing his new task, he was asked to be the dispatch coordinator for all the trash crews and pick-up drivers. His new obligation with the company required him to now choose which highways were in more serious need of attention and then assign the various crews to the areas of greatest priority. As to be expected, he landed himself another raise and greater trust and responsibility among his superiors.

I know I've chased a pretty long rabbit trail here but the point is, Carlos didn't get into the rut of complacency, consoling himself that he was good enough by comparing himself to the worst examples of men who surrounded him on any given day. He certainly had plenty of bottom-shelf, substandard men to measure himself against as he progressed through his career. Notice how I didn't say stupid men or wicked men. Just men who hadn't had their awakening moment yet and realized that it was time to level up and evolve. Carlos focused on self every day and if there was ever any comparing or competing, it was only with the man that he had been the day before. By making himself his own project, he was able to push past barriers and systematically excel in every area of life. He finished his parole, married a beautiful woman, bought a home, started a family and went on to become the chief operations manager for the entire program. He oversaw the highway maintenance project for the entire state of Texas. He had gone from eating dry ass pancakes in prison to eating lunch with state legislatures at the state capitol. He decided to finalize his resume of majestic accomplishments by returning to the very prison system that he started in so many years earlier and offering himself as living proof that *anyone* can come from *any place* of brokenness and destitution and fight through the self-limiting belief system, conquer the self-sabotage mindset and finally start crushing it in life and arrive at a place of unlimited opportunities. He did it. I've done it. Others are doing it. You can do it.

On the other side of that comparison coin lies the unhealthy danger of comparing up from where we currently are. Comparing down can afford you a false appraisal of where you're really at, making you feel better about yourself to the point where you slow down your momentum for personal growth and development. Comparing up, however, can leave you feeling overwhelmed because you understand at a basic level the amount of focus, hard work, time and dedication that it's going to take to get yourself there. Don't let the successful people around you discourage you from your journey. Don't adopt the mindset of "I could never be like that guy." In fact, you should surround yourself with successful people, for the well-known adage teaches, "You are the sum total of the five people who you hang out with most." Allow the successful people in your immediate sphere to inspire and guide you on your pilgrimage to becoming apex. Don't let what appears to be a life of ease and success for these people discourage you on your course. I know that for you it isn't easy or effortless to succeed. I'm sure some days it feels like you're charging hell with a water pistol to just simply stay sober. Nothing comes free and easy. However, it eventually becomes cheaper and more natural as we go.

The only comparing that we do in life is against ourselves. Stay hungry, stay committed, stay focused.

Actionable steps: Going forward, I want you to begin to get up earlier in the morning. In a quiet place away from distraction, no phones, no social media or interference of any kind, I want you to begin to visualize yourself being successful. What does that look like for you? Negative habits that you may need to kick. Positive habits that you need to develop and maintain. Obstacles and challenges that seem insurmountable now and how you can overcome them. I want you to write out on paper where you want to be as a man. What do you imagine in your mind when you imagine yourself at the top of your game, functioning from a place of success? What are the obstacles that are currently in your way? What habits are bringing you down? What success rituals do you need to implement in your life to begin to train yourself to start winning? What defeatism mindsets do you have that give power to that lying voice that exists within all of us that says "you can never win"? It's time to start becoming self-aware. Knowing yourself is the key to overcoming self-sabotage and creating a world-class life.

Also, I want you to ponder, during that early morning quiet time, these Webster's dictionary definitions of the word *awakening*.

1. "Rousing." As though a bear is waking up after a long winter's hibernation and realizes that he needs to thrive. The bear, at a base level, knows two things.

First, that he would love to just keep sleeping. It feels good. It's safe. He's comfortable. Yet simultaneously, he understands that if he continues this way much longer, he will die. He's groggy at first and fumbles around for a bit but very quickly, he gets focused and becomes the apex predator at the very pinnacle of the food chain.

2. "A revival or renewal of interest." A newfound interest in yourself and your overall well-being. Make concern for yourself and your overall health and wellness a personal project of upmost importance. Make attention to yourself and your condition as a man a daily priority. The practice of going from substandard to apex is a beautiful transformation process that should be considered parallel to the creation of an amazing work of art. Enjoy the developmental evolution of yourself as an Apex Man.

PRINCIPLE 2:

THE SELF-AWARENESS PRINCIPLE

It was February of 1998. I had just shot up a huge half-gram blast of crystal methamphetamines in the bathroom of the neighborhood gas station in Evanston, Wyoming. It was the first time in my history of meth use that I ever slammed dope that was made with ether rather than lighter fluid. It tasted like cocaine instead of the normal toxic petroleum flavor that

I had become accustomed to. As usual, I was already insanely out of my mind high before borrowing the bathroom at the 7-Eleven for another round of injections. I had this process down to a science. I would stash my dope before injecting; that way all I had to do was rinse my needle, flush my cotton, get the cap back on my needle and quickly leave the gas station before the intense rush of adrenaline and dopamine took over my entire person. I always knew it had been a home-run blast when my vision got blurred like the tracking on an old school VCR and I could hear the deafening, rhythmic whoosh of helicopter blades pulsing in my ears. I had been hitchhiking across the country for several years already. Searching for something, or someplace.

Searching for some type of new experience or stroke of luck maybe that would change the fact that I was completely bound in addiction to anything and everything that would alleviate a pain that I didn't even realize existed inside of me. Maybe I kind of knew there was something off, but I definitely couldn't explain or quantify exactly what it was. All I knew, in this moment, is that the helicopters were friendly and the shadow monsters were not. I hadn't eaten nor slept in days. No worries though, we had enough shandy glass to get us at least into Salt Lake City before that notorious and climactic event known as automatic body shutdown (ABS) took place. Only the more experienced and veteran road tramp tweakers like myself were able to time this event with being in a land filled with homeless shelters and soup kitchens. The Mormons were strict, but they took care of their tramps. The Greater Salt Lake Valley was a land overflowing with wealthy religious people who were committed to their ideology of feeding and sheltering the misfortunate folks that happened through their turf. And there were always some good day labor jobs available for a transient street rat to be able to scrounge up the next round of funding to re-up his dope sack and get him on his way.

Stepping out of the bathroom, feeling rightly medicated, the helicopters and I set out on our journey to nowhere in particular because quite honestly, until this dope wears off, I'm already right where I want to be ... Alas, we have to keep moving though, right? I had enough cognitive sensibility to know that I should distance myself from anyone human or pretending to be.

In this state of mind, humans were the enemy. Unpredictable, suspicious and always staring. The shadow monsters at least honored a set of rules. Yes, to be seen and heard with the occasional perceived malicious intentions but never actualizing any real harm toward me. They were my favorite part of the experience. As my usage continued and the sleep deprivation worsened, my self-induced state of mad hatter psychosis gave rise and intensity to the shadow people. Basically, the higher I got, the more of them there were and the more sinister were their perceived intentions. Hiding behind everything, whispering. Just loud enough to not be sure if they were even there at all. Occasionally darting out behind a bush or building only to vanish from my peripheral vision as quickly as they had entered it. As my meth-induced hallucinations intensified, I decided that an epic showdown between the shadow monsters and me was imminent. It was time to fall off the map. Yep, we were good and lost now. Let the games commence.

I knew that at some point, I would need to be near the highway but not close enough to attract any imperial entanglements. The railroad tracks that ran parallel with I-80 were set back about a mile from the asphalt. Seemed safe enough. I began my "trip." I walked for miles down those railroad tracks. Completely oblivious was I to the frigid temperatures associated with the now blizzard-like conditions that were escalating as the last remaining evidence of light vanished over an obscured horizon. Miles and miles of walking, talking to myself, yelling at the shadow people for not being as slick as they thought they were. I knew they were there. All around me. Hiding in the sagebrush, again whispering just loud enough to not be sure. They were really good at what they did. It's against the rules of the game for me to let them know that though. They must believe that I know that they are out there. It's only when they suspect that you're unsure of their existence that they increase their levels of malicious intent. I have to stay vigilant. There's really only one way to do that I suppose.

I called a time-out. It was obvious that I needed another blast if I was going to keep up with so many of them. Especially if it was going to get dark soon. Up ahead was a tiny substation next to the tracks. It was a little shack of a building less than six square feet in dimension. All I really needed was the illumination from the sickly yellow light emanating from above the tiny door on the outside. It's hard to hit a vein in the dark. As I reached my destination, I retrieved my needle and my spoon from my bag. Quietly humming that old hippy song by Janis Joplin about a harpoon and a dirty red bandana, I grabbed my dope sack and had the frustrating realization that I had no water in which to liquify my dope so that I could draw it back up into my syringe. Compounding this frustration was the irony that I was surrounded by tons of moisture in the form of snow and ice. Unusable. Damn. Not to be deterred, we decided to get primeval. My only option was to draw thirty units of warm blood from my own arm to use as the liquifying agent to get that dope into an injectable state. The wind was merciless. The light kept flickering. Somebody was lying on the roof of this building watching me, claws outstretched. Waiting for me to focus too intently on my task so that they could ...

It was such an inconvenience trying to get high in these conditions. I had the thought that I should call my local legislature and complain, but at this point, I didn't really know where I was or who to call. Had I crossed the state line yet? No way to tell for sure. Besides, cell phones hadn't been invented yet and the last couple of times that I tried to use my spoon as phone, it didn't work. Bad signal, I guess.

I decided to just do all of it. You know, just get it out of the way and be done with it. How much was left, you ask? Funny how that information is really important to at least half of the people who are reading this. I'll say this much; it was enough to open the portal. Only some of you will understand that and that's OK. There's an amount of meth that, once ingested, takes a person to a land where there are no rules; nothing is absolute. Time, gravity, common sense, and pain don't exist here. You develop your own fantasy reality depending on what's internally taking place within you at the moment. One truly crosses the threshold where the living and the dead coexist ...

Struggling against the elements and the intense scrutiny of my imaginary companions was too stressful. The coldness around me was starting to make my bloody concoction coagulate. Fighting the wind and my blurred vision, I finally landed the kill shot and ... I'll be damned ... the helicopters are back again.

As the chemicals entered my bloodstream, my body instantly became awash with the soothing warmth that every meth addict is familiar with but can't rightly explain. Like being tucked in with a weighted blanket on a bed of clean sheets pulled straight from the dryer. The euphoria starts in your head and quickly moves through every part of your person. There is nothing on earth that compares to this. Not even sex. I'm whole again. I'm well again. I'm ... sliding down the outside wall of this tiny brick shack to my ass, gasping for breath as my vision now turns kaleidoscopic. I see it. The portal is welcoming. Beckoning. Familiar. I can't move. Paralyzed by adrenaline and dopamine coursing through every fiber of my being. I don't even need to step through. The portal passes over me like an all-knowing entity, aware of my desire to vanish into the fray. In response to my actions, it condescends to my request, giving me entrance and access to the land of demented reality. Yes, we are now truly as far away from reality as anyone can be. I'm as far away from myself as I can truly be and that's the point of all this, right? I'm so thankful to be lost. I would very much like to stay right here forever. I cannot remember my pain.

It's pointless to try and keep track of time in a state of mind like this. Nevertheless, as my breathing resumed to normal and my head regained some sense of cognizant awareness, I felt the need to know what time it was here on earth. I'd never done a shot that big before. Where was I? Heck, who was I? Subconsciously, I knew at gut level to just fall into the high and let go of any unanswered questions about irrelevant issues concerning identity and geographical location.

I was now no one.

I was now nowhere.

This was what I signed up for, right? Yes. Indeed yes.

My companions had been gracious to me thus far. They always gave me a minute to recover before resuming the game. However, I could sense their malicious fidgeting was reaching a crescendo. They were anxious to begin again and I would need to be on my feet, in A-game mode very soon.

I had to know the time.

I decided to make a sundial using my spoon and the light from the iridescent bulb above the door on the train shack. I couldn't make sense of it. Was I supposed to face north? It didn't matter; the shadow kept spinning around the spoon like the second hand of a clock. Like the pulsing of a strobe light through fractured glitches. Best I could guess, it was two in the morning. Give or take three days ...

The shuffling impatience of the shadow monsters was now audible. Their whispers of impending doom and destruction were now modifying into a steady roar. There must have been hundreds of them. Their hatred for me was literally vibrating the ground beneath my feet. As I picked up my tools and readied myself for round two, I was struck blind by what seemed to be the light of a thousand suns all converged at once. Seriously, the entire prairie was lit up as though the stadium lights had come on all together at one time. Was this Judgment Day? I was toast. This is not the way to meet your maker. The light intensified just before the trumpets sounded off. Deafening. Dreadful. The brass instruments boomed off the landscape like cannon fire. Woe is me. I am undone. Weighed in the balances and found wanting. I fell to my knees awaiting those eternal and rightly deserved words, "Depart from me, you that work sin and iniquity, into everlasting torment." They never came ...

The ruggedness of the terrain caused a momentary bend in the curvature of the tracks allowing the floodlight on the train to point north. I could clearly see the silhouette of the engine as it barreled up over the hillside. The apocalypse wasn't upon me after all. Not cool, man. Didn't he realize that there were people out here trying to fight demons, heavily under the influence of psychotropic stimulants? Really, the nerve of some people. The engineer kept laying on that God-awful horn. Almost as if he was trying to send me a message. I didn't know Morse code, I couldn't read braille and I certainly didn't understand this archaic dialect of train siren. He was coming straight at me. All this damn room out here and he's got that thing pointed right at me. It took a second to realize that I had been kneeling on the tracks. Fair enough, I guess. I stepped off the tracks a few feet. Apparently, that wasn't enough room for his royal majesty because he decided to intensify his barrage of cannon fire across the landscape. What was he doing out here this late anyway? Only a very deranged human being would be out in the middle of nowhere, in Wyoming, in a blizzard at two in the morning. I pointed the handle of my utility spoon toward the train and spoke into the ladle. "Breaker fifty-seven eighty, do you copy?" No response. The towers must be down again. A few more unresponsive attempts to communicate before giving up and deciding to move on.

I elected to turn south, back toward the interstate and give his majesty all the room he so arrogantly thought that he needed. My heart stopped cold. The brilliance of the floodlight on the train had now lit up the savanna in all directions. There were legions of them. Uncountable thousands of shadow monsters that had formerly been obscured from my vision by the cloak of darkness were now exposed. Tucked in and behind every rock, every shrub. Every conceivable inanimate object on the terrain had become a hiding place for these mischievous bastards. I had the sinking realization that the helicopters had been quietly bringing them in all through the night. Parachuting them in under the cover of darkness. Could no one be trusted?

I admit that I panicked. There were just too many of them for your casual, run-of-the-mill game of hide-and-seek. Obviously, they were strengthening their numbers for a final takedown. You simply don't invest this kind of manpower without justifiable cause. The rules of the game were now changing. There would be no more time-outs. There would be no mercy. I needed a safe place and I needed it fast. The floodlight on the train had revealed my enemies. The floodlight was therefore the undeniable safe haven. I bolted down the tracks straight for the light as fast as my feet would carry me. Why is he laying on that God-awful horn again?

With the light from the train piercing straight into my eyes, it was hard to manage the ground beneath my feet. I hooked my foot on a railroad tie and tumbled off the tracks, ass over end through the sagebrush. I felt something squish underneath me, snarl and scurry off as I skidded face-first through the dirt. Don't look. Sometimes it's better not to know. I'm usually not one to harass inferior life forms during exoplanetary exploration. It'll have to get over it. Clearly, I have my own set of problems right now. I quickly stood to my feet in time to see the conductor hanging halfway out the one solitary window on the train. I couldn't quite make out what he was saying but judging by the look on his face and the way he was flailing his arms about; I could tell he was screaming out a level of vulgar and inappropriate profanity that would make even a submarine sailor ashamed to hear.

He must be in terrible agony. I could see no other reason for his dramatic display of charades. The demons had gotten into the train engine. I was sure of it. They were probably eating him alive from the inside or were starting on his legs and working their way up. Like a school of piranhas ripping and tearing his flesh from the bone in pieces. All of this just so I could see what would soon befall me. They wanted me in a state of abject horror before they devoured me alive. Poor bastard, there was nothing I could do for him now.

I grabbed my bag and hightailed it toward the asphalt.

There was another soft glowing, white light emanating from the freeway down below. I pulled my spoon out and flipped my wrist around a couple of times like I was opening a switch-blade or a butterfly knife. They needed to know that I was armed and dangerous. It might save me some time. Running full sprint down the hillside with my heart pounding, I could hear the siren getting louder and louder. They had taken over the train and jumped the tracks. I was sure of it. Any second now, they'd be driving that tank right over the top of me. I'm no Jason Bourne, but I knew at full sprint I could make the freeway in under six minutes. I was running so fast, I actually gained enough momentum to lift myself off the ground. The rhythmic pounding of my feet crunching through the snow came to a halt, yet my body still soared inches above the landscape. Unbelievable. I made a mental note never to buy dope in Wyoming again. Whose idea was this anyway?

My supernatural flight powers came to a screeching halt as I cracked through the ice of the frozen livestock pond that I had been sailing across. I wondered for a moment if they would follow me down here. I never got the chance to find out. The pond was only three feet deep in the center. With all the inertia that I had gained coming down the hillside, I actually flew out of the hole as fast as I had fallen in. Now face-first, ice burning down my cheek, I slid at breakneck speed toward the embankment that surrounded the circumference of the entire pond. How in hell did they manage to get in front of me? Crouching on the embankment, waiting, were three of the most unholy and grotesque shadow monsters I had ever encountered. Haggard and decrepit, hunched over with claws outstretched and fangs bearing with gleeful, ravenous hunger. So, this is how it ends, huh? Well, I wasn't going out without a fight. I aimed my spoon in the direction that I assumed would do the most damage. I *will* be remembered in the chronicles of the undead. My name will be whispered in hushed circles among the dark ones as a man who went out with respect and honor. My last moments alive will be spent dying with dignity, defending myself from the hellish fiends that sought my life and my soul.

Seconds before impact, I was brutally kicked in the face. I'd never been hit with such ferocity in my life. With my spoon aimed square and true, I closed my eyes as I slammed into the dirt embankment. At least three of them gored me with their horns, teeth and claws while I simultaneously drove my spoon wrist-deep straight through the torso, past the vital organs and clean through the spinal column of one of my assailants. A sickly, wet popping sound emitted as my trusty spoon ruptured through its backside. The bite wounds on my neck, face and hands were on fire. I lay there spent, heaving for breath, waiting for the venom to sink in and convert me to my rightful place among the ranks of the undead. Forever doomed to wander the open plains of southwest Wyoming looking for victims such as I was, to feed off their fear and stupidity.

Moments passed. Nothing. Just get it over with already! I couldn't move; I could barely breathe. Pinned to the ground, they were letting the apprehension build. At least I got one. Up until tonight, I don't think it's ever happened. *No one* has ever killed a shadow monster. The glory is mine. I will be remembered. They must be giving a moment of silence to their fallen comrade before the real torment begins. There would be no one to hear my tortured screams as they echoed across the prairie. I was in bad shape.

A break in the clouds afforded me the necessary moonlight to gain a more accurate assessment of my circumstances. Apparently, I had slid down the ice, slamming face-first into a cedar post before entangling myself in triple spur barbed wire fencing that surrounded the pond. All this coinciding in an instant as I drove my rounded shank straight through the wet center of an Escobaria cactus that was minding its own business at the pond.

I just lay there. True to rules, they never touched me. Their mischievous laughter was more felt than heard. Being drowned out by two final elongated bursts of a profane and obscene insult coming from the conductor who, just like me, had managed to survive his ordeal unscathed, as he and his train disappeared over the last ridge into the night.

I opted to yank the thorns out my hands and neck before untangling myself from the barbed wire. It wasn't the single strand stuff either. This sucked. Who did this to me? Freeing myself from my entrapment, I stood to my feet. I had the unsettling realization that they were never trying to kill me. They were only trying to get me to kill myself. Wow.

Grateful to be mostly alive, I hobbled the remaining forty yards out of the wilderness, back into civilization, and right through the front doors of the commercial weigh station for CDL drivers. The one solitary Department of Transportation officer on duty that night looked me over and got on the phone. The tumbleweeds in my hair and the blood running down my face, combined with the fact that my pupils were so dilated black that I must have looked possessed, were all the clues he needed to know that I was not in good shape. After a quick call, he asked if he could help me. I informed him that I had been trying to hitchhike out of Wyoming into Salt Lake City and got stranded. I asked if I could just warm myself for a moment before attempting to walk back to Evanston. He consented to my request. Minutes later, a highway patrol officer walked through the doors. Same scenario, same story. He also, I think as more of a favor to his fellow port of entry counterpart, obliged me a warm ride in the back seat of his patrol vehicle.

He asked only one question from the front side of the cage that separated the stoic chauffeur from his troubled patronage. "Where ya headed?" "Anything that's open," I responded. I just needed to be able to warm up, maybe get a cup of coffee and be in the vicinity of morning traffic that would soon be headed west into the great state of Utah. After a brief but calming twenty-minute ride, the door opened. I climbed out of the patrol car dry enough and thankful to back among the living. Our destination seemed familiar. Ah yes, this was the very same 7-Eleven that I had started this God-awful, psychotropic nightmare at just twelve hours earlier. How ironic. I had once again almost killed myself multiple times in an effort to get ... nowhere. Seriously though, overdose, train death, hypothermia, blunt force trauma. In that moment though, it was the most riveting, thoroughly enjoyable excitement that I had created for myself to revel in. My escape from reality.

Question is, what was I running from? Myself? My past? My wounds? Who knew, who cared? No one did and that in itself was all the more cause to run further and further down this darkening path.

I slumped down the brick wall outside of the gas station, coming to rest underneath the payphone. I could see the taunting dance of my antagonists flickering down the alleyway with the headlights of every passing vehicle. Mocking me, jeering and ridiculing my plight. Their seductive swaying enticing me to once again come out of the light and play. I'm good. I shall lick my wounds and heal. He who fights and runs away lives to fight another day. Eighty-five miles yet to Salt Lake, I hunkered down, kept a watchful hallucinating eye and waited for daylight.

By now, you're probably asking yourself, what in the hell does a story like this have to do with self-awareness. My question to you is, what had transpired in my innocent youthful years that would make a grown man believe that not only was this an acceptable life but a preferred one? Why was I so intent on altering my reality to the point where self-destruction was a nonissue? What was I running from? Why was I unable to see myself sober, successful and happy?

Thus far, you've made some great strides for your cause as you advance yourself deeper into hostile lands. You've expanded your influence and secured a few notable victories. As noted earlier, most men will never even engage themselves for the cause. The fact that you've even decided to elevate yourself out of substandard and toxic living is commendable in itself. As you begin to progress on the journey of becoming an Apex Man, you should know that your enemy gives up no ground without a fight. He is as experienced as he is ruthless. A cunning and calculating foe that will engage in the most detestable form of trench warfare that you have ever seen. A seasoned and skillful killer of men, an accomplished and competent assassin. Knowing his enemy, he sees his opportunity and deploys his deadliest and most destructive weapon. Who is this seditionist villain you ask? It's you. The worst part of you. He exists inside each of us. Waiting. Patient. A manipulative and deceptive adversary who waits for your weakest moments to capitalize on and ambush your life. What is his greatest weapon? Simply, self-ignorance. The antonym of self-awareness.

Self-ignorance is your greatest enemy on this campaign of becoming the most elite and successful version of yourself. Others may disagree and say that self-sabotage or self-limiting belief systems are your worst enemy. I would have those people answer me this one question: Why do you self-sabotage? Why do you even have a system of self-limiting beliefs? The first question should never be how do we stop self-sabotage but rather, *why* do we self-sabotage? Or better yet, what did we experience in life past that initiated the pattern of reoccurring self-sabotaging behavior that continually keeps us stuck in bottom-shelf, substandard living? Why do so many people, as soon as they start seeing some basic and limited success, pull the pin on a hand grenade and toss it into their own life? If we can discover what traumatic events from our past are the "first cause" or inception of our self-sabotaging mindsets, then we can put laser focus on healing those breaks in the neuro-programming. Just like the fiber optic repairman for the cable company will dig up, expose, and re-splice damaged wires so that there is no longer any disruption of service to the client. We also need to pinpoint from our past the origins of why our minds work as they do. We need to pinpoint what traumatic event or series of events took place in our childhood or adolescence that caused the initial break in the fiber optic cables of our mind that keep causing a disruption in service. Seriously though, have you ever wondered why that beautiful woman, whose kindness and loyalty are unmatched, will repeatedly choose bottom-of-the-barrel, lowlife and abusive tyrants to share herself with? A woman who, if she just had a simple paradigm shift in how she saw herself and the world around her, would realize that she's putting her health and overall happiness in jeopardy unnecessarily. What type of psychological malfunctioning is occurring in her brain that causes her to believe with every part of her being that she is worthless and therefore doesn't deserve the highest and best standard of man that exists in the world? What causes her to not only accept substandard men but to attract and prefer them? When the relationship ends (and it usually does) and she's finally free, everyone in her life who cares for her rejoices and breathes a sigh of relief before cringing in horror as they watch her, not too long after, go right back to the same jerk or another one just as rotten as the last. Why does she do this? Even when she has been made aware of the behavior, she still almost uncontrollably gravitates back to the same choice. Why is she unable to believe that there isn't any reason why she can't have an amazing life, enjoy a wonderful relationship with a kind, compassionate man who will work his ass off to provide an amazing life for her and her children?

What about the man who sobers up, gets a great job, meets a great girl and finally starts gaining some financial headway before relapsing and losing that good job by spinning off for a week, or cheating on that girl and losing her, or getting some high-end credit cards and drowning himself in high-interest debt? He'll usually spend six months to a year rebuilding what he tore down, get caught up, and just before he starts hitting a certain level of success, he will tragically and with certain dependably commit a behavior that begins the process of tearing down everything that he's worked so hard to achieve all over again. Almost as if he enjoys rebuilding more than he enjoys steady, uniform levels of success. Almost like the universe itself has put a cap on the level of success that he is allowed to achieve and if he comes anywhere close to that boundary, the internal mechanisms in the hardware of his brain initiate the self-destruct program. The reality is they both have subconsciously placed a cap and a standard on themselves and they don't even realize that, whatever it was from their past that they suffered through, it now has taken ownership of the internal programming to the extent that it now controls the emotional, thought, speech belief, and action process section of the brain. The way they see themselves and their worth now determines the reality they create for themselves. Because they see themselves as worthless and not deserving of love, respect or success, they actually struggle to be comfortable when they start seeing love, respect and success come into their life. To the point where they subconsciously create for themselves tragic conditions so that they can be comfortable with not only what they are used to but what they subconsciously agree is what they are allowed to have. Self-awareness would certainly help both of them discover why they're broken. Self-awareness would allow them to pinpoint what traumatic event or abuse, whether acute (onetime event) or chronic (repeated events), happened to them in their past to cause the reoccurring self-destructive patterns. Self-awareness would enable them to discover what their triggers for relapse and self-sabotage are. A strong and robust sense of self-awareness would allow them to see in real time, as it's happening, or better yet just before it happens, the cues and indicators that would let them recognize and modify their choices and behaviors before it's too late. Anyone can fall into the same bad decision once or twice in life. Usually people just recover and move on. They chalk it up to learning, make mental notes and never go near a decision like that ever again. Yet why is it that some people seem hellbent for leather to repeat the same mistakes over and over again? They've gotten so used to failing that things actually seem abnormal when they're successful. As weird as this may seem, it's actually uncomfortable for these people to be consistent achievers. I was one of them.

Some of you, as you're reading this are like, "Yes, that's me! I'm that guy who consistently throws a hand grenade into my own life just when things start going well. How do I stop doing that?" I would be doing a great disservice to you if I exposed the problem yet offered no solution for healing and restoration. So we will go deep and do what we can to offer some basic tools for you to implement into your own life so that you can not only heal from toxic and substandard living but, in fact, go on to surge past those success boundary limitations and demand that the universe provide all the raw materials that you will need to build an amazing life. As comical as that may sound, it's an absolute reality. The universe provides whatever the machine in your head asks for. They are constantly communicating, at wavelengths undetected by the conscious mind. Even while you sleep, there is a quiet discourse taking place between the internal subconscious spark within you and the central creation point within the heavens. Yes, it may seem like psychobabble bullshit. Yes, it's probably just poetic and really more psychologically- and biologically-driven than it is esoteric and mystical. However, I guarantee beyond a shadow of a doubt that, however you choose to see it, it's an accurate concept. As we go, I ask that you be gracious to me. I am going to attempt to explain with stories and in very basic layman terminology something that highly intelligent people go to school for years to try and learn. The solution is all that matters for us, right? I don't need to use any impressive psychological terminology to try and impress you, right? Commoners like you and me just simply need the light bulb in our heads to come on so we can take some basic, actionable steps toward growth and healing.

Self-awareness or metacognition is a higher form of thinking that allows us to be aware in the moment of not only how we're feeling but why we feel that way. Have you ever seen a young child at about nine o'clock at night just have an epic breakdown and start crying pitifully for no apparent reason?

The child has no idea that they are just simply exhausted from a long day of being alive and need some sleep. By the same token, have you ever seen a young child late at night while watching cartoons with their older siblings just get up and leave the room and even though Mom and Dad are distracted, the child will put themselves to bed? Self-awareness allows one child to recognize not only how they're feeling but why they feel that way and then simply make the next right move. Have you ever seen a non-self-aware parent yell and scream at a tired child for having a meltdown? Not only are they unaware of what's wrong with their kid, but they are also completely unaware of how stupid they look for yelling at a tired kid who just simply needs a nap. Self-awareness allows us to know what we're feeling, what we're thinking, how we're speaking and how we're acting as we're doing it. This is termed as "being present." In addition to being in the moment, mindful of how we're feeling, thinking, speaking or acting, a strong sense of self-awareness allows you to know why you're feeling that way. Not just recognizing how you feel in the moment but being able to discern why you feel that way. What happened in your life, whether recently or in years past, that causes you to feel, think, speak and act the way you do. Finally, self-awareness allows us to perceive what the soon-to-be consequences will be if we continue to stay on the same trajectory of our current level of feeling, thinking, speaking or acting. It's a past, present and future awareness that lets a person function in and make decisions from a level of maturity that animals simply do not have. Unfortunately, some people do not have it either. I was one of them.

Self-aware people understand that if, for example, they have a bad experience in the morning at work and their boss gives them a hard time, whether justified or not, and they allow it to sour their emotional state, it won't be long before their thoughts are negative and sour as well. Self-aware people excel at reasoning and place a blockade around the event and deny it further progression into their psyche because they know that soured emotions will produce and fuel soured thoughts. They understand that soured thoughts give life to sour speech patterns and soured speech patterns reinforce and initiate negative and toxic behaviors that carry undesired consequences for their lives.

Non-self-aware people will spend the entire day fuming over the issue and allowing the offensive nature of someone else to steer their thoughts to a place where they waste many, many hours imagining negative scenarios of self-loathing, revenge or even violence against their boss for hurting their feelings. Instead of affecting life, they have now just been affected by life.

Self-ignorance is a state of being in which the thought patterns of a person are unharnessed and uncontrolled. Their thought life often runs unfettered and unchecked like a litter of puppies that somehow dug their way under the fence while their owner was away and they now run free across town in all directions. They will most certainly place themselves in troubled or dangerous situations if they are not captured and placed in a secured environment. Have you ever been there? In that place where you experience a pretty significant event in life and if you're not careful, it can dominate your mind for a good long minute. Why is it easier to imagine negativity than it is positivity?

The mind is really good at creating theatrical plots of tragedy. Often it will embellish and exaggerate ideas beyond what they would ever actually become in real life. The universe isn't trying to kill you. Your boss, in most cases, isn't actually trying to fire you. Just because you and your wife are going through a rough patch right now doesn't mean that she's cheating on you with the divorce attorney that she quietly hired to clean you out. If we're not careful, gentlemen, we can allow by default our minds to run wild into some pretty unrealistic territory. The dirty little secret to all of this is we actually create our own future realities by what we allow our thoughts to be today. Let me repeat this. How you think today shapes and determines your reality tomorrow. If you really think your boss is out to get you fired, then you will respond accordingly and get defensive and be a jerk back because you know he's trying to get rid of you anyway. His response to you being a jerk is to let you go because you have a bad attitude at work. Yes, your boss initiated the altercation but he was only trying to sharpen your abilities as an employee so that he could consider you for a promotion later but you interpreted it as his complete disdain for you as a human being. Instead of seeing it as a moment to learn and grow in your trade, you perceived it as an attack against your character as a man and got defensive and served the negativity ball right back. The intended outcome is now forever lost because your inability to see correctly caused you to create a false presumption of your reality. Basically, your unchecked thought life deepened and worsened to the point where you created your own outcome. Creepy as hell the power of the mind, is it not? Your divorce was never the intended outcome. Nevertheless, you keep fuming over suspicion of her intentions and replaying every hurtful word that she has spoken to you. This lack of self-awareness concerning how your thoughts are progressively developing has caused you to expect her to leave and so you respond accordingly by returning the same level of garbage right back. Hours and hours of negative thoughts all day, every day, now crescendo into an epic outcome of loss and failure created in the studio of your mind. A self-aware man would understand that your wife most likely wants things to work out; she simply doesn't know how to communicate correctly because her childhood was just as toxic and traumatic as yours. Self-aware people are thoughtful. They are patient problem solvers. They excel at being able to go a few layers deeper than the issue itself to look for clues to solve what appears to be a complicated dilemma.

The science behind self-awareness is as absolutely mind-blowing as it is educational and empowering. What I'm about to share with you will undoubtedly change your life. There's a megalithic emotional boulder that you've been carrying on your back for many years, my friend, and when we're done here, you're going to lay it down and walk away forever.

The human brain is filled with billions of neural pathways. Connective transmission lines that allow for information to be passed across the most intricately designed computer system in the universe. This powerful computer sits neatly inside your wet skull and we're only just beginning to understand its reach and capabilities. The neural pathways start developing right away in the womb and accelerate quickly as life progresses. Neural pathways are created as we experience life through our senses. Sight, smell, sound, taste, touch and emotion are the sensual tools that let us understand the world around us. Every time you and I experience an event in life, whether significant or trivial, through one of these biological data collection devices, that information is then copied and pasted into a brand new neural pathway in your brain. This is mostly done for the purpose of self-preservation. For example, as an infant your body is craving nourishment in order to live. The discomfort associated with being hungry causes you to cry. Upon hearing the first few whimpered cries that emanate from your tiny lips, someone you don't really know all that well shoves a warm, rounded breast into your mouth that just happens to be filled with all the life-giving nutrition that you so desperately need. In that instant, a neural pathway is created in your brain to capture and hold that event into memory for the purpose of self-preservation.

Because your brain's ultimate purpose is to cause you to live, it will keep these memories that are now stored in neural pathways so that it can draw back on them again and again as needed to make decisions in the future on what to do if you are ever put into that situation again. Multiple pathways are created simultaneously for each event. Your brain not only created a pathway that said crying resolves the issue but it also, at the very same time, created one that said staying quiet did not resolve the issue. Over the course of your life, all of these pathways will connect to each other with transmitters along the way to help push information quickly, allowing you to make decisions that will keep you safer, stronger and alive. *Survival.*

So fast forward a few years and now, every time you cry, you get backhanded into a wall by a stepfather who wasn't previously in the picture but has now been recently introduced into the schematic of your life. Very quickly, from the purpose of self-preservation, your mind is going to develop neural pathways that will teach you through experience and memory to never cry and to keep ample distance from certain individuals. As a young child, you will now quickly become an avid student of body language, tone of voice, speech patterns and situational awareness. Not because you woke up one day and decided that those topics interested you, but because you now have to understand them in order to avoid pain and survive. If by chance as a child, you are on the spectrum even slightly or have ADHD or any other type of underdeveloped self-awareness or self-control deficiencies, then basically you're just screwed. There is a part of your brain that isn't firing in the normal processes that most of the rest of humanity does. Therefore, you don't learn as others do and struggle to avoid choices and decisions that are impulsive or troublingly inquisitive. If the response to your repetitive impulsive behavior is violent outbursts of rage or violence and demoralizing profanity, you will eventually become so traumatized that you become the actualized definition of the word *broken* |*broh-kun*| (adjective) (1) reduced to fragments, (2) torn, fractured, (3) not functioning properly, out of working order.

Every time as a child that you hear the words "you're a worthless piece of shit and you'll never amount to anything," every time someone you love packs a suitcase with your clothes and throws it and you out on the porch and says, "I hate what you're doing to this family." Every time you become a punching bag whether verbally or physically for someone else to vent their frustration and lack of self-control on, neural pathways are being created in your brain that tell you, through constant reinforced repetition, that you indeed are a worthless piece of shit and that you don't have any worth or value as a person. In the same way that Bill Gates or Steve Jobs will tell a computer program what its functions and limitations are, the software in your brain is being developed to consider certain axioms factual and undeniable. Namely, that you don't belong. That you're an inconvenience. That you're the root cause of all the sorrow of your family and the world around you. That you can't succeed. These are the lies that are being programmed into our heads as truth. As a child you don't know that though. So, as a result of the internal agony that develops from this mindset, we quickly learn tactics and strategies to cope with the ensuing pain. For me personally it was running away from home. I learned very quickly as a young teenager that I could survive on the streets of El Paso, Texas. If we got caught committing a crime, it was nothing more than a few weeks in juvenile detention, which in comparison to some of the garbage I dealt with at home, wasn't a bad trade-off.

Can you guess what the reoccurring theme, across all ethnicities and socioeconomic lines, was for every adolescent teen in that detention center? Yup. Good guess, my friend. Toxic and negative familial situations. It was a neglectful absence of positive masculine role models or abusive and demeaning parental influence. Every time. Always.

Other coping mechanisms for dealing with internal pain are obviously to medicate that pain with controlled substances. The pain, not being addressed or dealt with properly, never goes away. It just becomes deep-seated and permanent. Not being able to resolve the matter and heal is quickly replaced with the next best choice and that is to alter our reality by distorting it through illicit drug and alcohol usage. As mentioned earlier, narcotics, alcohol, porn and unhealthy eating disorders are primary creators of dopamine releases in the brain. This dopamine is felt and understood in the software as pleasurable and can be used to combat the suffering that, again, is not necessarily understood and quantifiable but is definitely felt and perceived. Over time, we not only develop a toxic perception of who we are but we develop an unhealthy coping mechanism to deal with this unrelenting, subconscious discomfort that never goes away. We only solidify the false assumptions that we're substandard and unsuccessful because there are real-time consequences that coincide with being an addict to these aforementioned addictive activities. With every bad choice, another neural pathway is developed, proving the evident reality that you are a bottom-shelf person and are incapable of making good decisions. Something that started outside of our control or desire for ourselves now becomes the coffin that we continue nailing shut with every subsequent septic choice that we make in life. Basically, someone else laid the corrupt foundation for a broken structure and you and I continued adding corrupt framework to the structure itself as we went through life.

So fast forward thirty years and a hundred billion negative neural pathways later. You are now entrenched in a mindset and lifestyle that every day reaffirms your apparent inability to function as a successful, positive member of the human race. You're cynical, dishonest, suspicious, faithless, impoverished, destructively impulsive, angry, addicted, perverted, overflowing with self-limitation, self-sabotage and fill in the blank with any uncountable number of other toxic and negative character attributes as a person. What now? If your computer had a virus that bad, what would you do? Toss it and start fresh? Go through the mainframe and systematically, one by one, eradicate over a hundred billion negative strands of digital code until you finally, hopefully before you die, manage to erase each one? What if I told you that the process for repair was much simpler than that? What if you could go back to that original infectious email that was laden with destructive strains of hardware damaging viruses and introduce a simple procedure that would eradicate every strand of malicious code that was introduced into your device? As unrealistic as that may seem, there are certain tools that exist in life that can assist in repairing the mainframe of your head to the point where you can heal from a broken heart and a broken past.

The first of these tools in the subcategory of self-awareness is "inception awareness." We have to be able to go back and discover or remember what the actual events were that started the whole process of becoming broken. In my case, I clearly remember at the age of four, lying in bed, almost asleep, my half-sister standing up in her crib screaming her head off because she was teething or hungry or just tired and didn't realize it. Just before I drifted off to sleep, the door to my bedroom was explosively kicked open and my stepfather was standing there, belt in hand seething with anger over who knows what and because of some trivial, inconsequential nonsense, he decided that not only was I the cause, but the obvious venting point for that unknown frustration. It's amazing to me how thirty-eight years later, I can still clearly see the outline of his frame, dark and obscured from the front and lit up from the back by the light shining down the hallway from the living room of our tiny Houston, Texas, apartment. The first of many little seeds that would be buried in the soil of my heart, teaching me my worth and place in the dynamic of a toxic family structure. What had I done? I was clueless. Obviously, I was responsible for something terribly wrong. Had I killed someone? Broken something? I was terrified. Would you believe that to this day, my lovely wife of fourteen years of marriage will not walk up on me in a dark room while I'm sleeping. She's only done it once. She will never do it again.

No. Contrary to where I left you in the last paragraph, I have never put my hands on my wife. On the contrary, what really happens is, I wake up in a state of uncertainty of where I am, in more of a lucid state of partial wokeness, sensing the shadowy outlined figure above me as I whimper, gasping for breath in a coward state of fear at the incorrectly perceived malicious intentions of my unknown attacker. Falling off the bed, struggling to wake up completely, I usually back myself into a corner, loudly cussing and crying myself awake. Odd, no? I've fought fist to cuff with the best of them. Throwing down ugly with cholo gangbangers on the bridge coming back from Juarez, Mexico. Awake, I have no issue with physical confrontation. Even if I know I'm going to lose. I find it rather sportive, but in that lucid, in-between state of consciousness, I'm that little boy again. Terrified. Unable to defend myself. Without defense.

I can remember a couple of years later, coming home from school with a piece of paper that said I had been rambunctious in class. Being a crime clearly worth public execution, I should have been grateful that my punishment was so light. Along with a slew of profane and demoralizing insults, I was lifted off the ground and thrown against the wall over the top of my bunk bed as the light switch was smacked off, followed by another sucker punch smack to the face concluding the affair that sent me to school the following morning with a black eye. I was seven years old.

I can remember being pinned to the ground with one hand around my throat and another hand clutching an expensive vase that was being brandished as the evident method of execution while hearing those seething with hatred words through clenched teeth that I was hated and I should be killed.

I remember having my shit thrown into a suitcase at eight years old and being tossed out onto the porch at night feeling unwanted, unaccepted and unloved.

I remember having my dinner plate placed on the floor

and being told to eat like a dog if I wasn't going to have any table manners.

I remember my father being a jerk to my mom and my mom realizing that if she mentioned my name and some pitiful slight infraction that I had made, she could deflect his anger off of herself and on to me.

I remember. The neural pathways that were created in those moments will forever be with me, not only haunting me but attempting to define me as a man.

I can assure you that I don't stand alone. I stand shoulder to shoulder with untold numbers of other broken people who have gone through similar or variant types of traumatic events in their past. The stories I've heard in juvey, on the road and during both of my stints in prison over the years are heartbreaking to say the least. People who watched their father brutally murder their mother. People who got off the bus from school and walked through the front door to find their mother dead from a heroin overdose. People who were sexually abused repeatedly by someone who they should have been able to trust. The inability to process these events for what they really are can, in many cases, cause us to blame ourselves and believe that we are the first-cause and responsible parties for all this heartache and destruction. Cementing further and in greater numbers the negative neural pathways that exist in our brain.

No longer. We are now waking up and realizing that the inception of our toxic and broken mindsets was not our fault. Think of the vast amounts of people who walk under a constant cloud of self-loathing and self-hatred like Eeyore, that depressed and pathetic old donkey from Winnie-the-Pooh. "Nobody loves me, nobody cares."

If you get nothing else out of this chapter, just know this. It's not your fault. Somebody messed you up really good and now here you stand. The resulting final product of someone else's toxic and negative influence on your life. Know this though, now that you're aware, if you don't do anything to fix the toxicity that exists inside you, you will relieve those people of their blame and place it squarely on yourself. Most likely, you will pass the same toxic garbage down the line through your kids and make twice the son of hell that you are.

It's amazing to me that after having come to some basic conclusions about all this and then implementing some patience and grace toward my son, who struggles with the same impulsive and slightly spectrum-centered behaviors, how increasingly positive and healthy is the outcome of his development. Basically, if you're willing, you can learn how to leverage every tragedy from your past and use it to influence yourself and others toward positive outcomes in every arena of your life. To accomplish this, we must learn to walk in a constant state of self-awareness.

I can assure you that going forward, just because of this information that you've now been exposed to, you will begin to become aware of yourself a little better than you are today. If you make it a point to be mindful and practice the art of self-awareness, you will strengthen this capability within yourself. When something negative is brewing inside of you for any reason, you will now stop what you're doing and take a few moments and ask yourself why you feel this way. You will also begin to understand where these feelings will take you if you continue to stay in them. Knowing the outcome of staying negative in your thinking and being able to see the ensuing consequences, whether it's a negative reaction that carries with it unintended fallout or simply wasting an entire morning dwelling on something unnecessarily, you will now catch and harness those naughty little thought puppies and redirect them through the use of certain tools. You will start being solution-minded rather than problem-focused. You will be more self-analytical and ask if there's fault on your end first before attacking the faults in others. You will seek out the reasons to be grateful in even the most horrendous circumstances so that your primary emotion in any situation is gratitude. This is apex human intellect functioning at its pinnacle point.

The following takeaways are a basic list of self-awareness practices that you can immediately implement in your life to start growing the self-awareness muscles that already exist inside of you. Never stop this practice. The moment that you do, you will again, by default, gravitate from apex metacognition back to animal instinct. As society progresses down the path of increasing mindfulness and enlightenment as a whole, there will be less tolerance for the animal man. He will become ostracized and find himself repeatedly falling prey to his own inability to evolve as a man. His inability to perceive his own circumstances for what they really are will keep him at the bottom in every area of his life. Discontent and frustrated, his only option for relief will be to continue increasing the stock price of Tennessee sour mash whiskey in an effort to numb his mind from the cold hard reality that he's a bottom feeder and always will be.

1. Self-awareness allows you to not only know what your emotions and actions are in real time, but you will also know what transpired, whether recently or long ago, to cause your current emotional/actionable state to become what it now is. Basically, instead of just being angry or sad, you will be able to know why you feel that way. You'll be able to connect the dots by analyzing the recent events of your week and put first-cause incidents in their place as to why you are now experiencing certain emotions. This level of self-awareness may not take away the feelings of anger, anxiety or sadness but at least you'll know why you feel a certain way. It's the confusion of not knowing why we have negative feelings that add to the chaos. In being able to understand and pinpoint the first-cause events that have triggered the negative emotions, you and I will be able to better create solutions to heal quicker and maybe avoid repeating the same circumstances again to save ourselves unnecessary headache in the future. In addition to past and present awareness of self, you will understand that remaining in any current emotional state, whether negative or positive, will always produce unintended consequences. When something negative happens in life, if we're not careful to guard ourselves against letting our emotions become soured, we will find ourselves becoming reactionary. Our responses to life's upsets will become impulsive rather than thought out. We will find ourselves

being affected by life rather than affecting life. Emotions are the catalyst for actions. Always. You will never escape this fundamental law of nature: if you stay toxic in your head and heart, very soon, there will be venom on your lips and blood on your hands.

2. Self-awareness allows you to not only understand the entire emotional/actionable dynamic of yourself, but it allows you stop just short of an impulsive response to other people's toxic behavior and analyze them and their actions to understand why they feel, think, speak and behave as they do. Remember our earlier example with the immature parents screaming at a tired child. As you become more self-aware and in tune with your own emotions, you will start to function from a place of patience as you evaluate other people's emotional responses, opinions, words and actions. It doesn't mean you have to agree with people's toxic behavior or moments of weakness that are revealed by how they carry themselves. It just means that you've taken the time to go one layer back to the root cause of why people are the way they are. If you caught a young child lying to you, instead of being impulsive and reactionary, stop and ask yourself, does this child get beaten at home every time they misbehave? That would certainly, from a self-preservation aspect, cause any one of us to mislead or misdirect people. On occasion, because your growing and using tools to heal yourself, you'll be better prepared to maybe invest some time into someone else, helping them heal as well. Slow the heck down and seek to understand or

you're going to continue setting our evolutionary process as humans back to impulsive, reactionary caveman days. If you don't figure this out, you're going to damage your kids and launch three more toxic humans into the gene pool. I know. I was one of them.

3. Self-awareness also allows you to express your feelings and their root causes to others. Not only are you seeking to understand other people and their junk so that you can afford them space, patience and grace, but you're able to share with others how you're feeling and why you feel that way so that they can give you space, patience and grace. Maybe, even on occasion, you would be able to get some information to help you heal. Wow. Wouldn't that be an amazing place to be in as a society?

   People at home and at work willing to just be brutally honest about how they feel and transparent about what they've been through in their past so that other people, from a place of compassion and respect on a very basic level, can afford them empathy. Evolving. Becoming ... Again, this type of behavior causes humanity to communicate and interact at higher levels. Very much needed in the world today. As you master this skill of communicating your feelings, you will be able to ask the right questions to other hurting people in order for them to be able to give voice to their pain. You are now, by asking the right questions, training other people to not only become more self-aware but how to communicate those feelings to others so that they can receive empathy.

4. Self-awareness causes us to understand that the negative neural pathways in the brain can never fully be erased. Yet, like any natural pathway or forest trail, we can create new ones to travel down and as we do this, the grass will grow over the old pathways, becoming a track that we frequent less and less. The creation of new and positive pathways takes time, but as we begin to prefer those pathways, we will overpower the brain with a completely new way of thinking and interpreting life. Eventually a complete paradigm shift happens within the neuroplasticity of the brain itself. Causing you to have a well-defined and robust network of affirming, confident, fearless, loving, healthy, patient, on and on ad infinitum transmission lines in your head. You now function at your core from a place of love and empathetic compassion for yourself and all of humanity. You now firmly believe that everything that the universe brings your way is for your development and your greater good. The positive mindset that now exists within you is connecting to the creation center in the heavens and making arrangements and diplomatic negotiations to now provide wealth, love, opportunity and fulfillment for your life. Don't doubt me on this. I now live it every day. You can too. Start believing in yourself. Start blazing new trails!

5. Self-awareness allows people to understand that when we cater to every whimsical desire that our carnal, fleshly passions have, we inadvertently train ourselves to be impulsive and without self-control. When we repeatedly

engage in dopamine-releasing, reward center of the brain arousing activities, we are literally creating new neural pathways in the brain for impulsiveness that will eventually begin to overpower the self-restraint capability center of the brain. Have you ever gotten into a tub of ice cream or a bag of Oreo cookies and lost track of time, misbehaving in a real bad way? Almost as if a mind-possessing parasite has completely taken over your entire person before subjugating your reason and willpower to its own scandalous and nefarious conspiracies. When it's all said and done, there's that slight twinge of shame, regret and embarrassment at your obvious inability to control yourself. Now imagine 100x dopamine chemicals being released into your brain when you use illicit narcotics to daily medicate deep-seated internal psychological pain that never goes away. Every time you use, you recreate and strengthen neural pathways for addiction that become the very core of who you are as a person.

Imagine a young teenage boy who lies in bed with his phone, watching porn and masturbating night after night. Whether it's boredom or self-medicating, the stress of simply being a teen, with each pleasure-creating, dopamine-releasing event, new neural pathways are created that not only force him to submit to that impulse with greater ease, but they actually create a core belief system for him of what is right and acceptable in the area of sexuality. Years later, when his wife tries to explain to him that she doesn't enjoy being tied up and horsewhipped in bed, he can't understand why, because for the last seven years or so, through repetitive engagement in sexually impulsive pornography usage, that's what he's conditioned the neuroplasticity in his brain to embrace and accept as normal. He has now incorrectly developed a false assumption that these lewd, abnormal and often sadomasochistic sexual positions and practices are acceptable and something that women prefer. Unfortunately, because of the toxic nature of this trap, the lewd and perverted passions must deepen in order for him to even be aroused, let alone climax. If not addressed, he will continue creating neural pathways that demand to be obeyed, screaming like an infant child that's starving to death and knows only to scream and scream and scream repeatedly until its petitions are met in full. Its only petition is to engage in whatever behaviors will release the greatest number of dopamine chemicals in the fastest way. Do it now and do it quickly. The consequences are irrelevant. Self-aware people practice a bit of self-denial from time to time to reinforce to self who is in charge. Practicing self-denial and self-restraint actually create neural pathways in the brain that communicate with the rest of the neighborhood up there. Broadcasting that, although we may have some ice cream from time to time, there is a responsible adult up here who will put the kibosh on anything toxic that's taking place and they'll do it very quickly.

6. Self-awareness allows us to understand what our triggers for bad decisions are. We all have them. Those moments in life where we're potentially in a weakened state and

more prone to be impulsive rather than self-controlled. A mature and self-aware individual knows what their triggers are so that they can avoid those situations as best as possible. As well, they also know that if a moment of weakness happens to occur, it's not because they are psychologically impaired. They learn to give themselves grace for the failures because they understand that they have a tailor-made, individualized set of personal triggers that are prone to get the better of them from time to time if they're not careful. The danger here isn't the occasional failure or lapse in best judgment. It's walking through life completely oblivious to what a trigger is and more specifically what your personal triggers are. The world is filled with people who walk in absolute unawareness to certain personal truths. They don't understand, for example, that simply being physically exhausted can be a trigger for relapse. I personally work six days a week, usually twelve to fourteen hours a day at my job in the oil and gas industry here in North Dakota. That's a normal oilfield schedule. If I'm not careful and attentive to my own physical chemistry, I can have a breakdown and carry myself in a way that doesn't align with my core values as a man. Usually by Thursday, I make it a point to come home from work, kiss all my peeps and be in bed way earlier than normal, making sure to hit the snooze the following morning just so that I can recharge myself and not be more susceptible to weakened moments of regret. Exhaustion is huge for me. I must be proactive and thoughtful, knowing myself and creating an actionable plan for trigger mitigation.

My wife knows that there will be one day a week where I'm going to address myself in a self-care fashion and get caught up, so to speak, and she knows the immediate and tragic results in temperament and behavior if I don't do triage on myself and heal.

No one, including myself, is demanding that I not let my triggers get the better of me. There's no demeaning finger being shaken in my face for having triggers and being susceptible to fall under their weight. Intelligent people just create and implement strategies for avoidance, mitigation, and recovery.

So, what are your triggers? Those events, emotions, experiences and feelings that place you in a more "prone to fall" position. How are you avoiding them? Sometimes you simply just cannot. We can't avoid the birthday or a death date anniversary of a loved one who passed away tragically and unexpectedly. You can't avoid a divorce anniversary. So how do you mitigate that dangerous situation that falls on the same date every year and makes you so depressed that you pound a bottle of cheap whiskey or wine to "celebrate" your grief? Do you involve friends? Family? Go out for a meal with people who you love and care for later in the evening so that you consume a better part of the night, "intentionally" distracted, keeping your mind occupied in a positive way. However you choose to do it, all I'm really suggesting here is, know your triggers for toxic choices and mitigate the hazards.

Let's look at a few others, just to give you an idea of other possible triggers that may be hindering you from being your most elite self. Again, this information can be very liberating because up until now, many of you think that you misbehave because you're permanently broken. I'm telling you that you occasionally misbehave because you have triggers. There's a difference, and it matters. I'm so tired of people walking around with their heads down, defeated and broken. Walking in a state of self-loathing because they wrongly think that they, and they alone, are inept human beings for being prone to fall under the weight of personal triggers. We all have them. Everybody. Even the best put-together people can crack and tumble if put into the right set of circumstances. Please start walking with your head up. It's an outright rule at our house. No one walks with their head down around here. On occasion, you may even hear my stimulatingly strong reminder to my kids: "You're a Chontos; walk with your head up."

As we go through this list within a list, be thinking about what your own personal set of emotional triggers are.

Is the negativity of the media a trigger for you? The constant barrage of hopelessness and defeatism can really be a discouragement to some. What steps are you taking to mitigate this new and extremely addictive substance on the market today, known as state-run media? Psst ... Turn the TV off. If aliens ever decided to come to our planet and watch the nightly news outlets for a week, they would pack up and leave just as quickly as they arrived. Many of us have just decided to turn it off completely because of the despair that one is left with after seeing how the condition of our world is portrayed by the nightly news.

It isn't an accurate assessment of what's truly going on around you. For example, you never hear that in America, two million people get married every year. You only hear that 39 percent of them get divorced. You'll often hear that every year 88,000 Americans die from alcohol-related incidents. Yet you'll never hear that on a yearly basis, roughly 36 percent of those people sober up and walk away from alcohol forever. That's an astounding 31,680 people who defeat a powerful demon and change their life for the good forever. Good news doesn't sell; bad news sells. It also fuels negative feelings of hopelessness in your heart. Hopelessness is a trigger for many. Learn to cut off the head of the snake. Turn your TV off, delete some Facebook friends and get around some positive people. Join the ranks of the many, many Americans who are now using their evening hours for better causes such as exercise, family time or furthering their education.

Is being overextended in multiple areas of your life a trigger for you? Stressed and busy often with too many activities and work tasks. Many of them trivial and unnecessary. Having too many things on your plate can often lead to not doing any of them very well because you're stretched so thin. The cold reality of not bringing your best to the table in multiple areas as a result of being stretched thin can make one falsely believe that they are a failure at life or at best underperforming and cheating those obligations of their best work. The ensuing, incorrectly diagnosed issue creates a depressive state in which every overextended soccer mom seeks to medicate in unhealthy ways to elevate out of the unhappy cortisol zone into the pacified and happier dopamine zone. Yes, calories are just as addictive as wine. Know yourself. Maybe it's time to let something go. Maybe it's time to take a break, focusing on the most important things for a while before resuming the busyness of life again. Some of you actually believe that if the universe gave you four more hours in a day, you could get it all done. You'd fill those four hours up with more horse hockey within a month. Once again finding yourself taxed, exhausted and overextended. Analyze your life. Make some hard choices and free yourself of the stress of being overbooked and drained all the time. For many, this pace is unforeseeably unsustainable. There is a titanic-sized iceberg in your future and when it hits, it will trigger bad emotional and physical states of being for you. It's time to write out some columned lists and prioritize the most important things. We don't need to be all things to all people. The strategy for being a successful multitasker is to get really proficient at the basics and then slowly introduce the extras, in increments, always making sure that you're not so locked in to anything to the point that you can't politely excuse yourself if the need to refocus on the more important things ever arises. This is proactive, thoughtful, projective self-awareness. Learn it. You can do this.

Is rejection a trigger for you? Rejection is a generic emotional response to several different first-cause experiences that a person may encounter on their journey through life. It can be caused by neglect or abandonment as a child. Children who have bounced from multiple different foster homes or that possibly have had multiple different parental figures or primary caregivers in their life may experience feelings of rejection. A young lady who I knew several years ago confessed to me that every time that her mom would split up with her live-in boyfriend, the loss of the masculine influence in the home would cause her to wonder if she had done something to make him leave. It made her feel fragile and broken. She felt abandoned and unlovable. If this unhealthy emotional trigger isn't dealt with, she, like so many other people, will carry this toxic mindset into her adult relationships and possibly put herself into an unhealthy situation where she will "do" or "tolerate" anything to simply keep a man from leaving her so that she can avoid that feeling of abandonment and rejection. For many people, relational breakups churn up those old feelings from our childhood where we either sensed or knew that we were an unwanted nuisance or inconvenience to someone who should have loved us unconditionally.

That's why it's essential to choose your relationship partners carefully. People these days are really quick to overlook the more important aspects of a person's character in their haste to climb in the sack or climb into a lease on an apartment. We just want somebody. Or maybe we just don't want to be alone. Our unwillingness as a society to validate relationship compatibility can bite us in the ass later on when things become so toxic that it's obvious that they can no longer continue. That's when someone makes the first jump off of a burning train without looking back. Tearing blended families apart, cleaning out bank accounts, violating lease agreements and ruining credit scores. Most importantly though, someone is always left feeling rejected ... again. Neural pathways in the brain being reinforced and created that say, "unaccepted, unwanted, unlovable, undesirable." The dirty little secret is it's not always the grown-ups that are wounded and scarred from this impulsive, repeated display of self-ignorant behavior. Kids can be wounded by the adult separation. Also, as the one parent goes into a mental state of psychological hibernation after the traumatic event occurs, they most assuredly neglect their children to the degree that the kids feel isolated and alone.

It's so easy to isolate our children. In more ways than one. Especially when our children are naturally going through some of those more annoying stages in life. If we're not careful as parents, our body language, choice of words and indifferent dismissals of our children will send a loud and clear message that they are not accepted, or worse, that they are not wanted or valued as a special person in our lives. Back to your stupid Facebook profile you go, to look at another irrelevant social media post by somebody with no real life as your child walks off quietly to their room fully aware of where your preferences truly lie.

Being bullied can be another trigger for rejection, and rightly so. People usually don't harass and abuse things that they truly value and appreciate. This was definitely a big one for me. As if all the bullshit going on at home wasn't enough, I was blessed to be a lanky, pimply-faced white kid who looked like Kurt Cobain from Nirvana on crack. I attracted so much unwanted attention from the gang-bangers and jocks in middle school. I was pushed around, threatened, talked down to, ridiculed and laughed at from what seemed to be every angle. Home sucked, school sucked, but I'll be damned if that first toke of weed in the ditch after school didn't make it all go away. Hmmm ... A neural pathway for dealing with pain was just created ...

Believe it or not, prison taught me more about how to be a real man than my father did. Prison is where I learned respect. Prison is where I learned to be willing to fight for my dignity, even when I knew I was outmatched and going to lose. Prison, and the older convicts who happened to stumble across my unlearned and ignorant path, taught me how to carry myself as a man. Those men taught me how to walk with my head up, not in arrogance but in self-assurance and a healthy sense of self-respect. It was my father's harsh words that tore down everything inside of me and sent me spiraling down a path of self-loathing and self-defeat. All of that had to be rebuilt from the ground up. If you're willing to see it, even your worst tragedies can be a blessing. I really needed those older, veteran convicts to take me under their wing and teach me a few things. The powers that be were willing to let me fall into that environment because they knew that not only would I get a time-out, but I would also get some much-needed discipleship on how to be a man. It was almost like a rite of passage in a way. Those older convicts, as tough and brutal as they are, had a soft spot for the younger guys coming in because they knew that we had been cheated, just like they had been, from a positive, affirming, supportive masculine influence. I believe those forty-year-old men saw themselves in us and decided to make an investment that might spare us the lost years and the heartache that was coming as a result of being confused and uncertain of who we were and what our purpose and place in the world was.

Criticism can be another rejection trigger. If you grew up in a home that was ripe, thick and plentiful of harsh criticism and judgment or absent of praise and affirmation, then anytime someone even remotely second-guesses you or questions your ability to make a good decision, it can dredge up those old feelings of inadequacy and rejection. It can trigger an emotional response that feels quite painful. If you've already discovered how to medicate pain through mind-altering, dopamine-releasing substances, then there will always be that pull to alleviate those unwanted feelings through whatever means necessary. Do it now and do it quickly.

Exclusion can be a rejection trigger for some as well. Feeling left out intentionally can make one wonder what might be wrong with them. When people purposefully leave others out of interactions or activities it once again, brandishes, with bold and bright colors, a neon sign that simply reads YOU ARE REJECTED.

Don't misread me, I understand that not everyone can

be invited to everything that goes on in life. As well, there may be real reasons why exclusion takes place. If you're a toxic person, then most likely, people are not going to want to readily include you into their routine. There's validity to that concept. All I'm trying to accomplish here is to create an awareness in you of a SITUATION that can trigger an emotional FEELING that causes someone to feel rejected. The end goal for me is not to decide who you include or exclude in your life, but rather to help you understand that rejection is a trigger that can make you feel undervalued as a person. Feeling undervalued as a person can make you want to medicate that negative feeling with negative behaviors that have long-term physical, emotional and addictive consequences. If people are leaving you out of things or seem to be uninterested in you as a person then you need to ask yourself why. The answer may discourage you but at least you'll have an idea of how to proceed so that you can attempt to repair that relationship if you choose to do so. Sometimes it simply isn't you. People are so lazy and so self-absorbed that they don't care to have interactions with others. There comes a time when you just have to let people go. Maybe it's for a season, maybe forever. You are now on a journey of becoming the most elite version of yourself that has, up to this point, ever existed. Don't beg people for their attention. Don't beg people to be in their presence. Don't beg people for their approval. Don't beg people for forgiveness. Forget those people. You don't need them. If you're truly trying to come up and out of toxicity, then you are, by nature in a different bracket of humanity, you are, in an elite club of exceptional, first-class people who are not only seriously trying to change themselves, but also positively affect the world around them. I know it hurts when you realize that, if you never called people or stopped by their house they would never reach out to you again. It gut punched me also when I did a little experiment last year and completely stopped contacting family and friends just to see who would respond or disappear. I want you to know it's part of life. Some of those people simply don't care about you. Some of them are so selfish and self-absorbed that they don't have the level of maturity, manners and self-respect to realize that if you genuinely care about people then you should reach out to them and tangibly express that care in a way that can be felt and seen. Also, there are some folks out there that are so distraught over their own lives and the current battles that they are drowning in, whether real or imagined, that they just can't get a moment out of their own perpetual tragic situation to focus and realize that they should show that they love and care for people. By reaching out and including people in their life through maintaining an actualized relationship experience, even if it's a simple text or quick call to check in with, or check on someone. It matters. It shows you care, and that simple act validates the true condition of your feelings toward the person and strengthens the relationship. We are just now starting to see the symptoms of the greatest epidemic that has ever truly plagued humanity. Social media has done nothing for society except create a painful social disconnect. The whole world now just stares at their screens. There is no intimacy anymore. Between friends, family, coworkers, all relationships have been impacted by the addiction of social media. As you progress, be mindful of this trap and rise above it. Finally, there are those people out there who feel so terrible about the things that they have done, whether to you or others, that they can't face the music. The guilt and regret that they deal with literally keeps them bogged down in solitude. They stay low profile because they don't want the reminders of who they were and what they did to others to resurface. They most likely have convinced themselves, for convenience sake, that you don't want to hear from them so they don't reach out. Don't let these people and the condition that they are currently in knock you down. Self-awareness simply lets you know that in most cases it isn't you; it's them. Give them grace and remember you need it too. However, do not beg *anyone* for their attention, relationship, trust or love. Apex people don't do that.

I would also like to inspire you to be extremely proactive and thoughtful with how you treat others around you. If these aforementioned people and their behavior can be a trigger for you then obviously, the next clear conclusion is that you and me and the way that we treat other people can either be a blessing or a trigger for them. Just like the toxic people from your past had a hand in creating negative neural pathways in your head, you and I, if we're not careful, can be the creative inspiration for starting some toxic and damaging neural pathways in others. Obviously, if you're reading this book, you are more than likely an adult who is trying to make sense of a lot of toxic junk that may be going on in your life. We can't change your past. We can, however, make sense of that past, give it some meaning and afford you some tools to grow and heal. What we cannot do, under any circumstances, is perpetuate the toxicity into others. One of the main reasons for writing this book is to stop the transfer of toxicity and brokenness into the next generation. You, my friend, can struggle through your brokenness and see immense levels of success and recovery, but please do not transfer any of that brokenness to your children. You already understand how difficult it is to try and sort through things in life as a result of what you endured. Spare them the years of struggle and pain and set them up for greater levels of fulfillment and success. Choose your words carefully.

Failure is another big-time trigger for people with mired pasts. When we grow up in an environment where toxic and destructive choices and behaviors are taking place, we get to experience firsthand the reality of failure.

Allow me to explain. When parental figures are making bad choices in life, they most certainly are attracting negative reactions and consequences as a result of those negative decisions and behaviors. Eviction, divorce, poverty, incarceration, health problems associated with addictions, depression and the list goes on and on. Young people growing up in these conditions get to see the repetitive cycle of adults trying to succeed, yet due to the poor choices that they continue to fall prey to, they always cycle back to outcomes of loss and failure. As jacked up as it may seem, the neuroplasticity in the brain of these young people will develop a mindset that tells them that this is a normal and acceptable way to live. In most cases, they will develop habits, addictions and decision-making skills that are parallel to what was displayed in the home. They too will, in turn, begin to live out the same cyclical pattern of trying to succeed and before attracting negative outcomes. They don't have any reference point for what success truly looks like. So they continue to engage in a pattern that's known, comfortable and understood. The unfortunate result is that they reinforce the belief that no matter what, even if they really, really try to break free from toxic living, it won't be long until another failure rolls around. Almost as if they expect it. Therefore, because of how powerful the mind is in creating the future realities that we experience, they will tragically attract, through belief, their next failure. The most unfortunate part of this whole process is that when they finally get tired of failure and substandard living and they start trying to succeed, when the occasional failure pops up, and it does for all of us, they will wrongly assume that they will never succeed in life so they give up trying. They incorrectly believe that they are predestined to always fail. This is an internal lie tightly embedded in the psyche. All of us will stumble as we proceed to live out the process of growing and maturing in life. The first couple of years are a bitch trying to get your act together. I can remember so many mistakes. The trick is to *never* give up in your attempt to succeed. As long as you're studious to learn and grow and you are committed to the *absolute truth* that you were not created to be a failure, you will mature and become successful. Remember, the reoccurring trap is that failures will trigger "worse after bad" decisions to medicate or alleviate the pain that's associated with having to look at yourself in the mirror after an epic blowout in character or decision-making. We must learn to tell that defeated little voice that we all have inside our heads that we are no longer a failure but rather we are a masterpiece of success on the journey to becoming the most elite versions of ourselves.

A famous quote by Thomas Edison, the man who failed miserably, hundreds of times before successfully creating the modern, mass-produced light bulb that brings light to billions of people the world over, goes like this: "Many of life's failures are people who did not realize how close they were to success when they gave up." Listen, you are closer than you think to mounting some of these obstacles and gaining some real traction in life. Don't quit. The worst part of you doesn't want to win. He's afraid of success because he's unfamiliar with it. Keep pressing. You were created to succeed. You will succeed.

Oprah Winfrey is another wild card success story that you may be unfamiliar with. Her mother became pregnant with her at thirteen. She grew up in an unhealthy, toxic family environment. She was sexually abused as a child and also became pregnant at thirteen. Something deep inside her at the core level got to a place where she said, "no more." She realized that failures and negative, sub-standard living were not going to be her story anymore. Against all odds, as a black woman in a society still trying to find its "racial high ground" and with what some would call a "mired," scarlet letter past, she rose above and built a reputation of success and wealth that now has her in the bracket of the topmost wealthy and influential people in the world.

While in prison, I got to see how prison tattoo ink is made. They take small, shredded-up bits and pieces of Styrofoam and plastic from the trash and they burn them in a pile under a hard, flat surface like the underside of a metal table or inside of a small commissary locker. Then they scrape the soot off the metal and add water and shampoo to the ashes to thicken it up a bit. I have seen some of the most beautiful, intricately designed works of art created by some of the most talented artists on the planet using the ashes of unwanted trash and garbage. Your life might seem like trash right now. Wasted years of sorrow and heartache that has you so weighted down in despair that you can't even imagine what a life of success might look like for you. I'm telling you now, with full faith, that your life can truly become absolute beauty painted from the ashes. I'm living proof. I know I've mentioned it before, but there was a long season of my life where I stacked up years of "worse after bad" decisions. There were years upon years of sowing stupidity and reaping consequences of loss and tragedy. It doesn't have to stay that way. It starts with belief. You must believe in the Artist and you must believe in yourself.

Purposelessness can also be a trigger for some. Although touched on briefly already, I'd like to go into greater detail about how purposelessness can cause someone to become discouraged and fall into old patterns and negative behaviors. We all have this sense within us, even at the very basic level, that we were destined for great things. I'm not necessarily saying that every detail of your life is preplanned outside of your own will. I'm simply saying that each of us has a call to a greater destiny than we truly understand. Sometimes we know what it is that we're supposed to do with our lives. Sometimes the clues and the opportunities unfold along the way. Either way, when we're stuck in bottom-shelf, substandard living, there's a part of us that knows that we're not living out our truth. Deep inside, there is a "knowing" that whispers and calls to us to get on the right path and start pressing forward in the right direction so that our lifestyle, character, and mindset can become practically aligned with who our "destined" self is. The destined self is always in the future, calling back to his past, which is your present today, to try and get us to align with who we're supposed to be, not who we were or who we currently are. I'm not saying that we can't enjoy the beautiful, almost magical process of growing into our destined self. We absolutely can and we should. There's no reason to wake up distraught every day over the reality that you're not that future, "destined self" right now. You will never be that future destined self as an exact carbon copy anyway, because every better decision that you make in life today sets him (or her) up better for their future tomorrow. Almost as if there's a supernatural hotline where your future self contacts you with petitions of desperation and encouragement to plead with you to make better choices now because they don't want to be the overweight, poverty-stricken, addicted, regret-filled person you caused them to become by the substandard choices that you are making today. They, unfortunately, will have less time than you do to try and fix what your unwilling "today self" destroyed through your indifferent, unwilling, defeated and careless mindset. The ultimate irony in all of it is that one day you wake up and find that you are no longer your today self. In the blink of an eye, in a hurried blur of time and pain, you discover that you have now become your future self and you now live in "real time," all the regret and loathsome heartache that your future self tried to warn you were coming. No legacy has been built, relationships are unrepairable, dreams, goals and ambitions unrealized and now, in many cases, it has become too late to try and pursue them.

Living without purpose is agonizing. Knowing that others are walking out their purpose and enjoying fulfillment in multiple areas of their lives while you quietly yet frustratingly stay stuck in stagnation can be so emotionally draining. Are you still stuck in the same dead-end job? Are you still stuck in the same negative and toxic relationships? Are you still stuck in the same rut of addiction to drugs and alcohol? Are you still stuck in a place of poverty because of impulsive, unrestrained spending habits? When we're stuck in substandard living, we place a blockade in between us and our purpose. We place boulders in our way on the path to achieving our goals and dream.

Living without purpose is a bitch. Here's why: For many of us, the toxic way in which we were raised and all the medicating that we do to alleviate the pain of a broken past coupled with all the "permanent" (not true) defeatism neuroplasticity in our brain has us almost enslaved in a lifestyle/mindset that doesn't align with who our future, destined self knows that we should be. We simply do not believe that we can be apex, destined people. Or, what I find to be most common is, we know that we should be, but we just don't know how to get there. It bothers us that the way we are constantly seems to overpower the way that we want to be.

When children begin the process of learning to walk, it takes time, progression and certainly a lot of falling, bumps and epic face plants. Eventually, over the course of time, the process is learned and mastered. Rolling over turns to crawling. Crawling turns to using the coffee table to stand up. Standing up turns to supported steps until we've walked the length of the coffee table before finally making the decision to step out into the "dangerous zone" of a carpeted living room.Most kids just have fun with the process of developing their legs and they don't get too bent out of shape about how long it takes to get there. My daughter Julia was not one of those kids. My wife and I began to notice toward the end of her "learning to walk process" that she was not real happy about the length of time it was taking her to figure out all of this upright, bipedal transportation. Sometimes, when she would fall, she would just sit there with her head down and look so sad. Almost as if she was wrestling with the idea that this might be a permanent outcome for her life. You could literally see the sadness in her eyes as she wondered to herself why everyone else in her life could walk and she couldn't. Obviously, she persisted and, ultimately, over the course of another month or so she developed her ability to walk. She had to learn, as an infant, to get up every day and continue trying. She had to learn how to not let yesterday's failures be a stumbling block for today's attempt at success. The process for growing out of toxic living and develop apex thriving is much the same way. We must be determined to succeed. We must give ourselves grace for the journey and not let the failures and the stumbles that will happen along the way to becoming a better version of ourselves hinder us from trying. Every day is a fresh piece of canvas to paint the rest of our lives on. If we're not careful, then we can subconsciously allow the stumbles to convince us that the goal of becoming apex is unattainable. Remember, Edison failed thousands of times before bringing the light bulb to reality. Michael Jordan missed nine thousand shots and lost three hundred games during his career. The reality of winning is simply determined by the determination to never stop trying. Personal growth and development is, at times, an ugly process. It can hurt. On occasion, we can hurt others. Especially when we stretch ourselves beyond our means and capabilities. It involves persistence even when life throws you curveballs. Even when the unexpected tragedies of life land in your lap, we must keep climbing. It seems as though the moment we decide to take action and take the necessary steps to change, the universe throws something at us to try and derail us. In those moments, we must have the right perspective. The universe will always test our resolve and determination in any field that we try to excel in. That's why so many people quit and never see the process through. They don't see the curveballs as growth opportunities. They see them as shutdowns or denials of achieving their dreams. What most people don't realize is that the universe has already agreed to support any decision that they make. Whether to grow and achieve or stay stagnant and live unfulfilled and substandard. If success and epic achievement were easy, then everyone would be successful and fulfilled. You and I know, however, that most people are neither. Why is that? Because they hate failure. They hate the stigma of trying to become something more than they are and getting pushback. They hate the feeling of trying to achieve greater accomplishments and getting their ass handed to them multiple times along the way. They value the comfort and safety of staying the same above the pain and frustration that can be involved with stumbling as they grow. They value their image and their ego of having the appearance of being put together and faultless as they live out their sad lives of quiet desperation.

Listen, even if you have a seriously traumatic past with

many things to overcome both mentally and emotionally, you can still find tremendous amounts of motivation to get up every day and continue on the path of purpose and success. Even on the darkest of days, even during the most difficult of seasons of life where everything in you is saying *screw this*, I'm done. If you have dreams and ambitions for your future and the future of the people who you love and care for, you can find the strength to get up and continue fighting to win.

Maybe we'll never be the next Bill Gates, Tony Robbins or Billy Graham, But I can damn sure guarantee you that you and I don't have to stay the same toxic people that we've always been. Who knows, maybe you will be the next Tony Robbins ...

I have big plans for myself. I would hope that you do too. I'm not currently qualified to be an instant success in many of those plans and ambitions that I have. Which of course means that as I begin to try and reach for those lofty, ambitious dreams that I'm probably going to fall flat on my lofty, aspiring ass more than once to try and get them. People will probably see me when I fall. I don't care. People will probably whisper in hushed critical conversations about how foolish I was to even dare to try such a lofty goal. Again, I don't care. I've got one life here to live before we head back to where we all came from. God's first command to Adam was to subdue the earth and multiply. Subdue your obstacles and start winning. Even if the whole world gets to watch you fail and fall repeatedly. I promise you will get to where you want to be in life. You will get to where you want be as a person. As you start to get close to becoming that person, destiny and *purpose* will be revealed to you. You will know why you're here and what your purposes are. I intentionally used the plural form of purpose because you absolutely have many more than one. I write this with all sincerity. You will become apex. You will find your purpose. You will impact the world in a positive way and leave your mark. I hope to run into you one day and hear your awesome story about how you overcame so much and realized your purpose and dreams.

Hopelessness is a kissing cousin to purposelessness and is almost certainly a trigger for many. When you've spent the better part of your life stuck in the monotonous, cyclical pattern of brokenness and substandard living, you can become overwhelmed at times with the false premise that you will never climb out. Your life can feel very much like a prison sentence even though you're not behind bars. The unending wave after wave of trials and tribulations, which are really nothing more than the "behavioral" choice seeds that your past self sowed into his future self, can pound on you repeatedly. As the megalithic waves crash on the shoreline of your tiny little island, you can hopelessly, yet incorrectly, assume that you'll never get a break in the waves to make an escape.

We can become so bogged down in turmoil that we begin to falsely believe that things will just always be this way. We inaccurately believe that we don't deserve success, fulfillment or true love and companionship. So we settle.

We settle for second- or even fifth-best and hunker down like soldiers in a foxhole on the front line of a losing battle waiting for the next barrage of gunfire to burst our way, keeping us pinned down until that fateful day when it all comes to a regretful end.

Nope. Not me, bro. I refuse. Are you coming with us?

You and I seriously need to start building a resume of little accomplishments that we can clearly see with our own eyes and hold firmly with our own hands. Something to reaffirm and reinforce the idea that we are capable of winning and that our future is, to a certain degree, in our own hands to do with as we please. When we start building a track record of winning, we begin to build new neural pathways in the brain that over time will outnumber and outmatch the negative ones. Remember, as we're building new ones and using them, the old ones become less traveled and therefore have less power and influence in our decision-making processes. They will also have less control over how we see ourselves and what we believe can be possible for our personal achievement levels. The new neural pathways will stabilize the idea that you deserve better and that you will have it soon. With each accomplishment we achieve in life, we are simply proving to that toxic, hopeless and substandard man inside of us that he is not us and that we are not he. Eventually he becomes converted to the idea that he is wrong and follows after, quietly in submission to the Apex Man. Finally, the two become one. When that happens, you will become free of self-sabotage and self-limiting beliefs. At that point in the game, there are no longer any limitations. Anything is possible. Because you finally have come to terms with the reality that you were created to be apex. You are simply resuming your place and purpose as was intentionally designed. Healing from the trauma and breaking free from the negativity is much like the butterfly breaking free from the cocoon. When you emerge, you are sound, aware, courageous and wholly unrecognizable from who you used to be. You wake up every day loving life, loving others and the world around you. You will see every obstacle as an opportunity to stretch and grow stronger in your new identity. Please come with us; please resume your original destiny. Life handed you a rough start; there's no denying it. Many uncountable millions of people will stay there. They will justify staying mediocre by blaming others. Only a small few in comparison will dig deep, find courage and leverage their broken past to achieve epic greatness and fulfillment. Will you be one of them?

Shame is the by far the most debilitating trigger that I would like to touch on. In my humble opinion, this emotion is by far the deadliest trigger for all people but especially for men. Much like an assassin who places a pillow over our faces as we lie sleeping, shame has the potential to exponentially suffocate all the courage and self-confidence one needs to stay ambitious and focused on the task of reforming themselves and evolving into the better man.

Let's get real for a moment, shall we? Forever with us is the memory of the wickedness that our hands have committed. Forever with us are our memories of the most despicable actions and choices that we have made over the course of an entire lifetime. Much like the neighborhood bully, these recollections of deplorable deeds can taunt us with accusatory reminders that seek only to persuade us that we are nothing more than deadbeat, reprobate losers who have no right to ever see ourselves as respectable, responsible men. We remember the people who we physically hurt and the sheer terror that was caused, leaving them psychologically traumatized for the rest of their lives. We remember the women who we've objectified sexually, taking advantage of their insecurities and using them for no other purpose than what some would consider a semen receptacle. We remember the innocent people who we abandoned like dirty rags in the trash because our addictions and self-centered lifestyle were more important at the time. We remember the moments of inflamed sexual passion where we committed acts of perversion just to bring ourselves to a pleasurable climax. These acts of selfish deplorability and wickedness flash like neon lights across the front of our minds continually. We manipulated the weak. We had no regard for the emotional trauma and psychological scarring that would forever haunt the people who we left with wounds so deep that they may never recover. We chose, time and again, the gratification of the flesh over purity and integrity. We have undeniably made many choices in life that have violated our core beliefs as men. We are now stuck in this awkward place where who we want to be isn't who we've been.

As men, we understand at a base level that a man is

defined by his actions, not his words. A man isn't apex because he wants to be or because he says he is, but because he behaves like one. As we ponder the actions of our past, we often see a scale tipped so heavily to the toxic that we can't find the belief within ourselves to see ourselves as quality, standup men worthy of the definition of being apex. We only see the failures. Therefore, we choose to submit to the idea that we're substandard. We choose to submit to the idea that we've faltered too many times to justly qualify for the chance of being considered a decent man. We forget so easily that there are honest reasons that brought us to this place. I don't seek to minimize the wrong that we've done. I'm not looking for a pass on my mistakes. However, I think it would serve us well to understand that many of us are a product of our upbringing, or lack thereof. Many of us missed, whether it was our fault, someone else's fault or an unfortunate mix of both, the lessons and the affirming encouragement that's needed to learn how to make better choices and deny the negative ones. I own my mistakes. Entirely. Yet a kid can't tie his shoes unless you train him how to do so. Not by screaming at him when he doesn't do it right, but by bending down close, with affirming, encouraging words and showing him. If you missed some training on morality or self-control or compassion growing up, it's going to reveal itself in your actions as you mature as a man. Why are you going to hate yourself and permanently label yourself as a lost cause because of all your mistakes in life when you were cheated of the privilege of being taught how to make better choices from a source that should have prioritized the training? It's like kicking a dog for chasing a cat. Unless there is rigorous, loving, patient, consistent training for us, we will always behave and make choices from our natural default mentality. Which will always be carnal, selfish, fleshly.

Believe it or not, I still struggle with this myself. Tremendously. The idea that what I've done is so bad that I'll never recover. Have you ever heard that voice? The one that says, "There's no coming back from this." The voice that says, "You will always be known as ..." (fill in whatever negative descriptive term applies). Why is there a part of me whose only purpose in life is to convince me that my reputation is forever shot with no hope of ever being repaired?

Much like those old school cameras from the 1800s that used gunpowder to burn images into paper to create a photo, every misdeed of my life is forever burned into the fabric of my memory. Haunting me, seeking to define me as a man.

As it relates to the conscience of man, we would do well to remember that if our thoughts trouble us from time to time about our past decisions, it means our conscience isn't seared. That's a good thing. It means that we're sensitive to right and wrong. The men who have let go of all conscience are the men who no longer care for what's right and wrong. These are the men who have completely abandoned their moral compass and have now reverted back to the primeval course of humanity. These men function from a mindset purely devoted to self-exaltation and self-gratification. They are without concern for the well-being of anyone or anything around them. That isn't us. That isn't you. The conscience is designed to convict the heart of man concerning his actions. This is a universal law. The goal is to create emotional discomfort so that the next time we are faced with an opportunity to make the same toxic choice, there will be the remembrance of that emotional discomfort. The brain at base level is constantly trying to pursue pleasure and avoid pain. Hopefully, the emotional pain that we feel after making bad choices outweighs the pleasure that we feel as we make them. That's why it's essential that we learn the art of "practicing consequences." This involves using our self-awareness muscles and playing out in our minds all the negative effects of the choices that we make, before we make them. Allowing ourselves to feel the pain of our convicted conscience before we make a bad decision can help steer our choices on the front side, before those choices are made.

Where the conviction of guilt turns ugly and begins to hinder men from succeeding in life is when that conviction turns into condemnation. Both words are legal terms that almost bear the same meaning. Yet, there's one striking difference. *Conviction* means a formal declaration of guilt. *Condemnation* means as a result of that guilt, there is now a permanent disapproval of the guilty. We want the conviction. I need my conscience to prick me when I'm making bad choices. I need the emotional discomfort that a pricked conscience brings in order to help steer my future choices. What I do not need, and what no one else is demanding of me is that I be condemned. God doesn't condemn people. People condemn themselves. That's a resounding truth found all throughout the scriptures. The condemnation that we feel oftentimes is a result of growing up in a home where our parents were so demeaning with their words that after every misdeed done, we were pronounced guilty and left to feel permanent disapproval from the powers that be. The powers that, at the time, were the only ones that mattered. As we age into men and get out from under the care of our parents, you would think that the voice of condemnation and permanent disapproval would go away. Not so, my friend, and here's why. Remember our past discussion on the neural pathways of the brain? How they're developed over decades to accept certain things to be true even though they are not? After having spent several decades being conditioned to believe that condemnation is the proper response for dealing with your infractions in life, you now carry that condemnation with you into your adult life. You now, impulsively, almost mechanically place on yourself the same level of "permanent disapproval" that your parents did when you were a child. This is also why many of you instinctively, yet incorrectly, assume that your Creator has also placed on your life a divine, irrevocable sentence of permanent disapproval.

Listen, my friend; it's time to make a choice. He is either love or condemnation. He is either compassionately fanning the flaming candle of your life or he is pinching the wick to vindictively extinguish you. He cannot do both. He cannot be both. It would violate his very nature. You just need to come to terms with this truth. You are loved beyond measure. You've been given a green light to come back from all this pain and toxicity and achieve immense levels of personal peace and success in life. Be careful; how you see yourself is how you assume others will see you. Maybe you should start seeing yourself as he does.

Don't believe me? Find a man who grew up in a home where his misdeeds were met with loving discipline followed by clear and well-felt restoration and acceptance and you will have the picture-perfect example of a man who can be convicted of his mistakes yet get up without feeling condemned for those mistakes and go on with his life almost as if nothing ever happened. He's made amends where he could but even if he never gets an opportunity to make things right, he's made amends with himself and he will never be bothered again by what he's done. He values himself enough to continue the journey of growing and learning how to be the better man. He understands that there is a quiet power all around him cheering him on to get up and go forth toward his destiny. However, the man who was left to feel that he's worthless and that he'll always be this way is the man who will always be condemned within himself; he will always revert back to the same toxic choices in a fruitless attempt to medicate the emotional agony of condemnation. He has no reason to try. Only winners try. Only winners get second chances.

He's not a winner. Somebody reassured him of that often enough over a long enough period of time to make it an unarguable, nonnegotiable fact.

I can hear the clunking sound of jaws dropping to the floor in shock as the light comes on upstairs. I can see the hamster wheel turning in their heads as men come to a better understanding of why they walk under a constant cloud of condemnation and defeat. I can see them go self-analytical as they begin to analyze their own parenting skills. When your kids make mistakes, deal with it however you wish; they're your kids but you better restore them afterward or they will slowly begin to build a billion neural pathways that cement in their heads the idea that condemnation is the proper emotional feeling that they should experience after every bad decision that they make. Even after you're dead and gone, your crippling voice of condemnation will forever live on inside their heads, making sure that they stay pushed down to the floor with every bad choice that they make in life. I don't know about you but shame and condemnation, at least for me, usually end up being dealt with by a stiff drink or a sharp syringe full of "forget me sludge." You decide.

As we wind down this list within a list concerning triggers and self-awareness, I'd like to leave you with a final trigger for bad decision-making. Negative associations can have more influence and sway on how people behave than some would like to admit. However, there is conclusive evidence to the contrary. If you are trying to come out of negativity and toxic, substandard living, then why would you ever want to remain in close proximity to people who are not like-minded for personal growth and development. It has been rightly said that we are the sum total of the five people who we hang out with most. When a person finally makes the decision to change their life and begin the process of letting go of the old ways and the old mindset, they must understand that they can no longer have a relationship to people, places or things that bear association to that old life. By nature, we are all able to be influenced. Even the strongest of us can feel the pull to yield to being less than we should be, especially when we're surrounded by it on a daily basis. Not only do we need to let go of people who are not committed to walking out this new direction in life but we need to find new people who are on the right path so that we can allow ourselves to be influenced and inspired to become what we are committed to attempting to become. Don't just ditch the negativity but surround yourself with positive, affirming, apex direction mindset people. It will speed up and solidify to a greater degree your own journey of evolving into your destined self. Changing your network is essential to becoming your best self but, likewise, we must make certain that we don't frequent places where we will be reminded of that old life. Don't feel obligated to meet your old friends at the bar to talk with them about personal growth and development. Don't feel obligated to go visit old comrades or even family members who you know have not yet had the awakening moment to try and convince them of their need to understand and embrace what you now understand and embrace. They must have their own awakening moment as you and I have had ours before you'll be able to have any real influence. The greatest influence that you and I could ever have in helping the people who we care for to wake up and move in a positive direction will be to live it out ourselves for a good season of time. We must develop a proven track record of being what we claim we now are or we will have no influence at all. We must distance ourselves from all negative influences as best as possible. This will allow us to develop the testimony of a changed life. When they see the reality of what is possible, I guarantee you that you won't need to go looking for them. When they're ready, they will come looking for you. When people get tired of the cold, they look for warmth. When people get tired of floundering in the darkness, they will run toward the light. Let's make sure that we're solid when they come. I know letting people go can feel like you're abandoning them but their greatest hope truly is that you will let them go and become apex. If not, you will both perish. I have an old associate from my lost years who I peek on from time to time. He and I used to be very close. He has spent the last twenty-five years in and out of rehab and sober living homes. He has lost so much time stuck in this cyclical pattern of being sober and then falling off the wagon hard. When I watch his Facebook posts, he will mount up this courage to sober up again but he never lets his old homies go. He continues to listen to toxic music and go places that are clear reminders of the old life. This behavior inadvertently allows the subtle influence of people, places and things to keep just enough of the door of hell cracked open that the first time he has a bad day or faces a serious trial, the influence of relapse and bad decision-making is so close, it's just a natural reflex to push the door the rest of the way open and let the enemy right back in. Close the door, my friend. You know what you need to do. Do it or die.

Now, let's continue with our self-awareness list and what the defining characteristics of self-aware people are. Several of these have been lightly touched on already, but we're going to revisit a few of them and give some examples as we go into greater detail.

7. Self-aware people are not reactionary. When they have a financial trial or setback, they don't immediately run to the payday loan business downtown and get themselves further into debt to solve a temporary problem that could have been resolved another way. They don't take out high-interest credit card loans to create quick-fix solutions to the financial trials that we all face in life from time to time. Debt is a monster obstacle to becoming successful in life. You should shy away from this type of behavior at all costs. Maybe they just need to come and repo that expensive vehicle that you should never have financed to begin with. Maybe, with some hard work and time, you can climb out of your hole in a way that, yes, may require some pain, but ultimately it will see you grow in the area of financial restraint. We all need to try better at living beneath our means.

The financial system is rigged. It preys on reactionary people. You never see the wealthy playing the lottery. There's a reason for that. And you never see people who are swamped in credit card debt enjoying true financial freedom. For most of us, wealth is a steady game. One that's played over time. It certainly doesn't need to take forty years to accomplish but very few people in life ever truly see immense levels of wealth just come to them overnight. Debt is like a living creature in that if he knows that you will welcome him, he will try to cause events in your life that make you more willing to invite him in. Only when he knows that you're opposed to unnecessary debt at all costs will he pack up and leave in search of a more willing and easy target. I say unnecessary debt because there are justifiable forms of debt. You certainly need a reliable vehicle to get yourself to work but are you financing a $40,000 pickup truck that's going to leave you swamped in a $700 monthly payment? A move like that will always keep you just short of your monthly needed intake. Financing a home can be a great investment for yourself and for your family, but if you're not ready for that mortgage payment and you constantly run up short every month trying to keep from falling behind, I can assure you that you won't experience the joy that owning a home can bring. It will become a curse.

Reactionary people are the ones who often end up doing or saying things that they regret later. In heated arguments, they use words that can do long-term damage. Although these reactionary outbursts can be apologized for, they can't be retracted. The saddest part of uncontrolled speech is that sometimes we can spew venom and we don't really mean it. Words often hurt worse than physical pain and the effects can last so much longer. Let's consider ourselves for a moment; would you not agree that most of the issues that we struggle with in our lives today stem from psychological trauma? Not to negate the physical abuse or treat it as irrelevant; no doubt all of it had a major role in shaping our brokenness today. Yet for me, when I look back on all of it, it was the words. The venom of ignorant people who in their anger or frustration would hiss and spew out hateful words to a young impressionable mind. Even when we try and make up for those uncontrolled outbursts of speech with kind words or kind actions, it can never erase the permanent neural pathways that were created when we lost control and let our poisonous fountain flow into the vessel of another. We must learn to slow down and take a deep breath or two before any words are spoken or any decisions are made, especially when they involve the potential to bring greater outcomes of pain and trouble into our lives or into the lives of others. Many a prison across the world is filled with people who simply didn't slow down and think things through before making a decision that changed the course of their life permanently in an unwanted negative way for years to come. Remember, reactionary people are constantly being affected by life instead of intentionally affecting life. Self-aware people make life turn out, mostly, in a way that they want and choose. Their life is seen by them much like a chessboard that requires setting up pieces well in advance and sticking to a strategy that leads them to a preplanned, desired outcome. When the heat is on, they don't panic and drop out or make plays out of fear or anxiety. They endure the pressure, slowly developing and implementing the proper moves to continue toward their desired outcome. Self-aware people are measured. Non-self-aware people usually end up tying themselves in knots. You'll often hear them utter phrases, like "Why did I buy that?" or "Why did I say that?" or "Why did I eat so much of that?" Instead of enjoying the confidence that's built from restraining themselves and making the better choice, they seem to live in a constant place of regret for being impulsive and uncontrolled in their decision-making. Living in a state of constant regret keeps them mentally defeated and it reinforces the notion that they can't succeed in life. It's a vicious cycle that strengthens itself over time.

8. Self-aware people practice the art of thought control. All of us, from time to time, can find our minds wandering in an unhealthy direction. It isn't so much that our thoughts wandered to begin with; rather it's the amount of time that we let our thoughts wander, what we let them wander toward and most importantly, are we even aware that our mind is even wandering. Whether it's of a sexual nature, a vengeful anger, or an anxiety-induced fear, if we're not careful, we can find ourselves creating and entertaining self-imposed theatrical plot lines of negativity. If we stay in that thought process long enough, it can actually create

neural pathways that compel us to incorrectly believe that's who we are or that's what our situation really is. Once we have convinced ourselves to any certain conclusion, we usually end up behaving in a manner that brings about the reality of what we've convinced ourselves of. If we allow our minds to wander profusely in the area of sexually immoral activities, we'll soon find ourselves craving and seeking at any cost the fulfillment of what we let our minds race toward. If we allow the offenses of others to make us mentally fret and fume in bitterness and rage for any length of time, we will soon create a hatred for those people who might make us behave or speak out of character. If we let discouragement or doubt run rampant and unchecked in our thought life for any length of time, very soon we'll be frozen up in fear and uncertainty. These negative traits fight powerfully against our ability to see ourselves successful and winning at life. When self-aware people find that their minds are wandering in an unproductive direction, they understand that the consequences of this mental chaos will immediately begin to permanently pollute a mind that they've worked so hard to build back from the brink of toxicity. They understand that their mind can transform the ether around them and literally create undesired outcomes that they'll regret later. They guard the condition of their minds as if it were a precious treasure. They understand that the mind is much like the story of the goose that lays the golden eggs. As long as the mind is in good shape, there will always be another golden egg coming. They understand that the mind and the shape that it's in can create immense levels of wealth and success for them. The mind is the creative power source for every person on the planet. It's where our ideas for success and opportunity come from. If your mind is healthy and unpolluted, it can inspire you to create something that can change the course of history. It can keep you focused and attentive to opportunities that you might have missed otherwise. Opportunities for wealth, love and fulfillment are dependent on the condition of our thought life. It can make you keen to opportunities in business, investments or partnerships that could potentially have the power to change the trajectory of your family tree forever. Having a sound mind gives you increased levels of discernment. Having a sound mind will give you the strength and determination to press through the tough seasons in life and not let barriers sideline you from achieving your goals. The mind is much like a powerful magnet that will attract back to itself outcomes and circumstances that reflect whatever condition the mind is currently in.

Thought life control is a developing practice. It can be difficult, especially in the beginning, to even catch yourself wandering in your mind. The habit of negative thinking cannot be reformed overnight. Remember, your thinking processes are a direct result of years of developed neuroplasticity. It literally is the core of who you are. There are, however, tools and methods for increasing the speed at which we build new neural pathways in the brain that will allow us to have a different worldview. This will allow us to make better decisions and attract better outcomes for our life. Positive affirmation through the spoken word is truly one of the most powerful rebuilding tools that one can implement in their life to see increased levels of growth and maturity in their walk to becoming a better person. I wholeheartedly suggest a full immersion in this practice. The more technical term for this strategy of mind healing is called NLP, neurolinguistic programming. Much in the same fashion that every negative word and experience that happened to you as an adolescent caused the development of a toxic mind, positive and affirming words coupled with positive and affirming experiences can completely reform the mind toward a positive and productive life. The trick is to saturate oneself in an atmosphere that is plentiful with the consumption and absorption of healthy content that will be received through the physical sense of hearing and transformed into belief. This reformation in belief will happen naturally over time. As I began my journey years ago to altering my entire worldview and personal belief system, it required me to be adamant about prioritizing my daily intake of positive and affirming subject matter. The only problem that one will face with incorporating this regimen into their life is finding and prioritizing the time to indulge in this practice. The content is out there. Listening to podcasts, watching TED Talk videos on YouTube, attending religious meetings, frequenting addiction recovery meetings or even seeing a therapist on a consistent schedule can create a massive and dynamic shift in how the mind processes, perceives and acts on any number of different situations that one can experience in life. For me personally, I chose to immerse myself in a lot of informative content concerning the area of childhood trauma. I also listened to many podcasts that dealt with "rags-to-riches" type true-life accounts from real people who started out in life psychologically broken and pulled themselves up to great levels of success and fulfillment in life. Over time, devouring this type of content, I re-formed the neuroplasticity in my own mind to begin to see myself as limitless in what I could achieve. I begin to realize that I could actually leverage every tragedy and setback in my past as a learning event to propel me to a better understanding of myself and the world around me. As I became informed and convinced of the science behind the psychology of how the mind works, I was able to become comfortable in my own skin. I was able to give myself a lot of grace for the journey. Grace is nothing more than "room to grow." I was no longer being held under the weight of a false notion that I was unrepairable. I was also able to make the connection that I was not the primary cause of why I've been broken for so many years. This was an empowering truth that gave me permission to not wallow in self-loathing and self-hatred for the occasional mistakes and failures that happened along the journey of becoming my better self. We must refuse the lies that all of us have just accepted to be true about ourselves. We can come back from brokenness. We can heal from childhood trauma. We are not resigned to accept the idea that we will always be toxic and defeated in our inner man. We must combat the lies with truth. The truth is, regardless of how unable to see it or believe it that you might be, you are an amazing person who should be liked and respected among your family and peers. The truth is success and fulfillment are all inclusive. They have no prejudice. Anyone, regardless of race, nationality, upbringing or status, can attain immense levels of success. There's no prerequisite required to being allowed passage to the destination of success. Only that you believe it's possible. Do you believe it's possible? It's time to evolve. It's time to become apex.

9. Self-aware people are also avid practitioners of the art of self-image projection. Self-image projection is an awareness tool that allows you to be mindful of how other people are perceiving you in real time so that you can adjust your attitude, speech or decision-making processes in order to create your desired perception of yourself in the minds of other people. It's OK if you need to read that last sentence again. Basically, instead of just being or acting as your normal self in every environment that you may find yourself in, you will now stop and consider where you are and who you are with and strategize how you want to be treated and what specific outcomes you would like from the people and circumstances that you're currently in. After you decide what your desired outcome is from the present circumstance or people with who you're engaging, you will morph into the correct avatar personality and carry yourself exactly as you need to so as to see an actualized manifestation of the end goal results that you either need or want. Sometimes what you need

or want will simply be the ability to be perceived by the other person in a way that gives you influential power over them for the purpose of speaking positive, encouraging words into their inner man in order to help them grow and succeed in life. This powerful self-awareness tool isn't just for selfish purposes. It can just as easily be used to develop and extract the greater qualities out of another person for their own good just as much yours. Yet we must know when and where to be which avatar. It takes a higher level of discernment and self-awareness to know when to flow in and out of the right personality character traits to achieve the highest level of success in your attempt to influence the people and circumstances around you. As an example, I personally enjoy making my wife laugh. I think that laughter is good for the soul and most people don't get enough of it. My wife internalizes issues a lot more than I do and she can find herself stressing over things unnecessarily. Usually, they are things that are out of her control or sphere of influence. So, I've commissioned myself the title and position of being that guy who reminds her not to take life too seriously. Thus, I often find myself intentionally projecting a type of goofball, silly, unserious image toward my wife. The problem with this image of myself that I can quite naturally flow into is that if I take that goofball clown to work and be that guy at my place of employment, I won't be seen as someone who takes their job seriously and therefore when serious, responsible positions become available or important task are required of someone, I will be the last person to be chosen for those tasks or positions. By not altering my image projection to a responsible, mature and task-focused individual, I hinder my own ability to move through the ranks at work and gain promotions and the financial increase that often follows those advancements. There's a place and time to be serious. There's a place and time for the jester. There's a place and time for brutality and there's a place and time for the romantic lover. It's not disingenuous to flow in and out of the many different archetype personalities that you will need to succeed in life because they are all you. As Ariel Hudnall so accurately describes in her blog on masculine archetypes, you are the Ruler, the Caregiver, the Creator/Artist, the Jester, the Magician, the Outlaw, the Hero, The Sage, the Explorer, the Lover and anything else that you need to be in any given circumstance in order to affect and manipulate your desired outcome for your life and the lives of those who you love and care for. As you and I start evolving as men and growing in the discipline of self-awareness, we must understand that self-image projection is a powerful tool that can really help us on our journey to becoming more confident and successful in the world.

Allow me to explain further what I mean by self-projection. A few years back, I was really starting to become introspective. I started looking deeper into the results of what building a reputation of being substandard accomplishes for one's self. I discovered that when everybody in your life expects you always to lose or disappoint them, they quit giving you opportunities to succeed. However, when people have an image of you as successful and capable, they will often seek you out to assist them in bringing important endeavors to fruition. If someone sees you as a bottom feeder that doesn't know their ass from a hole in the ground, not only are they not going to respect you but they're not going to seek out your advice, approval or assistance with anything in life. However, when people do respect your life, they most definitely will respect your opinion and approval of the choices and decisions that they themselves are unsure of. The result of this is that you now have the power to influence people and the choices that they make in life. Which means that you now have the power and influence to affect outcomes in people's lives in a way that's positive or that may benefit you in the long run. Bottom line with this is that people need to see you not as you truly are but as you want them to see you. You and I need to carry ourselves in a way where we are actively molding and shaping what others people's perception of us is. The whole world could be crashing down around us with stress mounting from all directions, yet if we're visibly calm and collected, other people begin to see us as strong and enduring. Even though we might feel like we're moments away from a catastrophic meltdown, as long as we're mindful of how we're projecting ourselves, we can convince people that we're standing tall, unshakeable and collected. Deceptive? Maybe, but are there not other aspects to our lives that we keep hidden from people?

I have a great friend back in Colorado. He's one of those really rare friends who actually take the time to stay connected and looks for the opportunity to display his friendship in a tangible way. You know, one of those guys who will come and help you up after you relapse and make a complete fool of yourself. One of those guys who will buy you a forty of malt liquor and make you swallow a couple of sleeping pills so you can put an end to a self-induced meth bender. The kind of guy who will put you on his couch and make you eat and go to sleep before you leave. His backstory is much like ours. I won't go into serious detail about everything he's done or endured in his life but I will tell you that whatever people may think of him, it's because he has premeditatedly gotten into their heads on the front side and developed their perception of him. No one who knows the man has developed their own perception of him. He has developed their perception of him by stopping and asking himself, "How do I need to carry myself in front of this person right now so that I'm allowing myself to be seen by them the way that I want them to see me?" Instead of just being his default self in every situation, among every person he meets, he proactively portrays himself in a specific way to influence their perception of him. Manipulative, you ask? On the contrary, I say ingenious!

At work he carries himself as he needs to, in order to create a perception of himself to his employees that allows him to maximize his influence and control over people and circumstances that arise on the job. In his marriage he carries himself differently than he needs to at work because he needs his wife to know that he cares for her and that he's supportive of her. He understands how he needs to portray himself as a husband to maximize the quality of his marriage and inspire his wife to be the best version of herself. At work there are deadlines and expectancies that he must meet and maintain in order for him to remain in the senior position that he's currently in. Sometimes this requires a heavier hand than one would use at home with his spouse or his children. At church he's willing to become the servant and be used in a ministry capacity if the need arises because, again, his desired outcome is ultimately for the success of the church. Every archetype personality that he chooses to flow in is always for the success of the organization, individual or relationship. Obviously, it's for his own success as well, and that's perfectly acceptable. This gentleman is apex self-awareness being displayed through the art of self-image projection. Over the years, he has learned to project himself in every arena that he might find himself in, in a way that allows him to widen, alter, affect, persuade, guide, impress, manipulate, regulate or shape not only outcomes but most importantly, perceptions. Manipulation has always had a slightly negative connotation to it. Yet, if you can manipulate someone to believe in themselves and behave accordingly, then is that negative? Start evolving, my friend. We're waiting on you.

My first real lesson with this came during my first hitch in prison. As unfortunate as it may seem, racism and tribalism are very prevalent inside those prison walls. Even though there were many similarities among the different races that united us, the contrasting cultural differences that exist between them are enough to where it's just difficult to associate with people outside of your own race. The Mexicans were very clean, very quiet and always seemed to be strategizing for power. The African Americans were oftentimes very loud and focused on sports and epic domino tournaments that were equally as loud as they were long. The Caucasians seemed to be always on the weights trying to catch up in size to everyone else. If white boys were gathering up, it was usually to pound iron on the weight yard or exchange recipes for cooking crystal methamphetamines.

While on the Middleton Unit in Abilene, Texas, I was in my dormitory with fifty-six other convicts, all of us waiting to go through diagnostic evaluations, which would ultimately determine where we would all spend the remainder of our sentences in the prison system. It was ninety days of boring visits with psychiatrists, physicians, and other prison administrative staff members. The agenda was to ask lots of questions and gather enough personal information about you to determine things like were you a gang member, were you a sexual pervert, how much time did you have in total, how many times had you been to prison already or were you violent and prone to psychotic episodes. All of this info would help them in their determination of whether you would go to one of the many minimum, medium or maximum security prisons scattered throughout the state of Texas.

While awaiting my transfer orders, I had struck up a friendship with an older convict who was obviously white like me with the same type of criminal history and addictions to meth and booze. We were just kindred spirits if you will. The only difference was he had ten years on me and was quite buffed out from lifting weights during his repeated visits to prison over the years. We would tease each other with inflammatory and derogatory insults just to mess with each other and make the time pass. One time in particular, I clearly remember calling him a pretty vulgar insult, one that we had tossed back and forth to each other on multiple occasions. This time, however, he jumped up and got right in my face and said that he was about to knock me smooth the heck out if I ever spoke to him like that again. It was intense, unexpected and completely sincere. Obviously, I was caught off guard by the response and chose, in the moment, the flight portion of the fight or flight response. I apologized for the infraction and said I didn't want any trouble and walked off. I could feel the cold, calculating stares of about five or six other inmates who happened to be in the vicinity of the altercation as they followed me back to my bunk. I sat there for a long while, not sure what had taken place. We had always played with each other like that. Why the sudden change in temperament and response?

A few hours later, he walked over and sat down at the edge of my bunk and explained that he had no problem with me whatsoever, only that I had put him in a precarious spot by insulting him in front of other people. He clearly told me that he was in a prison gang called the Aryan Circle and not only was he being watched by gang members from other gangs, but he was also being watched by people in his own gang. He said he couldn't allow other people to see him be spoken to like that. As long as we talked trash between us and no one else, it was fine. My first experience with self-image projection was intense but it made perfect sense. He needed to be seen as the type of person who would destroy on command without warning and for minimal causes. If anyone else saw me talk to him like that and realized that he wouldn't do anything to defend his honor, then in very short order, the whole prison would be talking to him like that and he would not only have no respect among the inmate population, but his prison gang would seem weak as well. At that point, he would be in trouble with them. It was a two-edged sword. I forced his hand by not being aware of certain unwritten rules that existed in the prison system. Lesson learned.

Consider with me a moment on how self-image projection works with our children. My biggest struggle with image projection among my own kids resides in that we as a family are the silliest bunch of pirates that we know. It's difficult for kids to take you seriously when it seems to be circus time, all of the time. Yet, we need to be serious from time to time and it's important to find the balance in how we project ourselves in our leadership roles because if we're goofy all of the time, then when those serious moments come around, you're going to find yourself pulling your hair out trying to get your younglings to take you seriously. In most cases, you'll end up having to explode into a tyrannical outrage just to get the message across that you are indeed serious. You and I can't blame the kids for not being able to discern the times and seasons when they fluctuate so much or lean heavy to one side.

What about the guy who's super clingy with his girlfriend all of the time? By being this way, he projects himself as codependent, insecure and immature. Those happen to be the qualities in a man that women despise the most. It's no wonder his love life is anemic and unfulfilled. What is he to do to alleviate his burden and see a healthy, positive turnaround in the response of his lady? Should he carry himself uninterested and detached? That, I dare say, wouldn't help his circumstances either. No, he must learn how to flow in and out of different states of personality as the need arises and as a countermeasure to however his girl may be acting in the moment. He has to know her and personify whatever archetype personality is required at the moment to gain the proper response from his woman that he needs. By doing this, he also provides the type of man, moment to moment, that his lady needs. Self-image projection always gives him the edge in any environment. One minute his girlfriend knows that he cares for her deeply and will provide for her every need and a second later, the guy harassing her at the park will know that his days are numbered if he doesn't back the hell up and get down the road. From lover to hero. From brutality to jester in a moment, with ease and sincerity because each archetype is fully you.

We've all been told over the years to just be ourselves and not worry about what other people think. It's time to eradicate that unhealthy bit of advice and start considering how other people perceive you. Have you ever walked into a room feeling confident and immediately had people start asking you your opinion on how things should be done? Almost as if they are naturally submitting to an authority that they perceive seems to emanate from you. On the other hand, have you ever tried to speak up in a room and had people talk over you and pick apart everything you say, almost as if they know that you're weak and inadequate? It's all about how you're projecting yourself. There's an ancient proverb that speaks directly to this; it reads like this: "Even a fool, when he's quiet, seems wise." Watch how you speak. Watch how you act and watch how you make decisions and respond to life's challenges. Like it or not, every day, depending on how we choose to carry ourselves, we are assisting other people in the development of their perception of us. If we have that much involvement in how people regard us, let us be diligent in making a good show of strength under fire, wisdom in choices and integrity in all aspects of life.

10. Self-aware people are influencers. The dictionary defines influence as the capacity to have an effect on the character, development or behavior of someone or something. Influencers are usually very confident people who know how to motivate and manipulate others to arrive at a predestined conclusion or outcome. Self-aware people also understand that impressionable people can be easily influenced with minimal effort. Listen close, my friend;

there is a conspicuous absence of solid, confident, masculine leadership in the world today. You and I don't even necessarily have to be the most alpha male personality that we know. As long as we can carry ourselves as confident men and be mindful of how we're being perceived through self-image projection, we can quite easily gain the attention of the people around us in a way that allows us to influence the character, development or behavior of those people.

As men, if we're solid, we have tremendous powers of influence on the people around us in every arena that we may find ourselves in. We have the power to influence our wives to become the type of emotionally secure and confident person that we would want our daughters to become. By the same token, if we're aimless and immature or uncertain of who we are and where we're going as men, we can influence our wives to be emotional basket cases. From a traditional marriage relationship perspective, your wife is really trying to let you lead her and your children in a positive, successful direction. When we're not emulating self-confidence and wisdom in decision-making, it can influence our wives in a negative way. Not only will your wife be lacking in self-confidence and peace of mind but she may begin to build a quiet disdain and frustration with your leadership and decision-making skills to the point where it can have a real negative impact on your marriage.

However, we can, if we're confident, have pure motives to lead and model care-based leadership skills at home with our spouses; we can influence them to be the best versions of themselves just as we are attempting to be the best versions of ourselves. You can inspire your spouse to lose weight and exercise, contributing to her overall health and happiness. You can inspire and influence your wife to level up her parenting strategies and skills to be the best mom that she can be. You can inspire and influence your wife to dream big and achieve great goals and ambitions for herself in her career. Listen, bro, don't badger and browbeat your wife. It's childish and immature. When a man comes home from work and projects this perturbed, displeased and dissatisfied manner to his wife because his life sucks and he doesn't have the courage to fix his own circumstances and fight for an epic solution to getting where he wants to be in life, then he's really just manifesting his own childishness. What a sad and pathetic relationship experience that must be for your wife, to be a homemaker, laboring for your home life experience, nurturing your children and washing the skid marks out of your britches to have you come home and project this bothered, annoyed and "vexed by her presence" aura.

You picked her, my friend, now saddle up and make it flourish. Start with some positive, affirming words. Tell her how grateful for her that you are. Ask her if there's anything that you can do on her behalf to empower her success in whatever she's doing on behalf of your family. Be kind and carry yourself with a level of self-assurance that bleeds out to her in a way where she can rest in your self-confidence and find her own. Whether she's homemaking or nine to fiving it in the workforce, use your natural masculine influence to make her the best that she can be. I guarantee that if your wife feels appreciated and confident in herself, it's only going to help you long term.

As fathers, we have immense levels of impact and influence over our children. As hard as it may seem to hear, whatever condition, whether good or bad, that our kids are in is a direct result of our diligence or negligence as fathers. Are you inconsistent in your disciplinary tactics? That's why your kids are a mess and don't consistently behave. Your inconsistency produces inconsistency. Have your kids given up even attempting to entertain a relationship with you? How much time are you personally spending on devices and shooing your kids' attempts at connection away like a pesky little fly trying to land on your watermelon slice? Is your son spending hours locked away in his room watching porn, having stroke marathons and who knows what else? Where are you, Dad? Did you have the talk? Are you willing to fight the fight? Or just let the chips fall and hope that you don't raise a predator. Are your daughters seeking out the attention of shady characters simply because they don't get yours? Are you willing to let that play out and simply hope that your daughter doesn't end up with some douche bag meth addict who just wants her flesh for his own carnal and sadistic passions? When is the last time that you encouraged her to have higher standards? When is the last time that she saw higher standards in you and realized that there was even such a thing as higher standards? You don't have to be white-collar wealthy to raise confident, classy and responsible kids. You just need to emulate a confident, caring enthusiasm that influences them to be solid. They need your time, yes, but most importantly they need to know and see that you are solid. Your son can grow up and not be a slave to every fleshy passion that he has. Your daughter can grow up and value herself and have a tremendous level of self-respect that lets her make better choices and have higher standards. It's never too late to influence your loved ones to succeed. By now you understand the seriousness of the matter. Your effort as a husband and especially as a father can change the course of history for multiple generations of people. It's bigger than maybe you've ever cared to see. Influence them for the good. This is a great work. More important than the overtime, more important than the UFC game, more important than the sale or the promotion. Insecure children grow up and waste what could have been. Insecure children are the result of insecure, unengaged, indifferent fathers. Evolve. Please.

The power of masculine influence knows no boundaries; its tendrils reach into every fabric of society, including your place of employment. As a man working in a man's industry here in the frozen tundra oilfields of North Dakota, I find myself surrounded by a certain breed of man. This type of labor-intensive and elemental-intensive work only attracts the strongest of men. Sixty below temperatures in the winter very quickly weed out the committed from the casual. Yet, even among the barbarians that labor in this financially lucrative industry, I still run across men who are hurting, lost, disenfranchised and aimlessly wandering in search of something that has less to do with money but more to do with a mindset of how they see themselves.

Allow me to share a story with you on the power of influence.

About twenty-five years ago, I was living homeless in a small city in the Midwest. I was either bouncing from couch to couch, living in abandoned houses or on the rare occasion living with one of my meth dealers in a motel room. I was part of a ring of thieves that was selling stolen property to the local cartel in exchange for dope. At this point in my journey, I was probably at what you could say was the lowest point in my life. I recall one time in particular where tweakers were getting so "out of their minds" crazy that guns were being pulled on people for getting behind on even the smallest of dope tabs. I remember being in the front seat of a car and having a gun pulled on me from the back seat and having my life threatened for a hundred dollars worth of meth that I wasn't even responsible for. At the same time, the Feds were breathing down our necks and getting awfully close to connecting all the dots and making an official round-up of everyone who was involved in our little theft scam. The heat was on from every direction and it was only going to be a matter of time before I was either back in the clink or dead. It was at this point that I decided that I needed to get the hell out of Dodge and find some new surroundings that were a bit safer to be in. I was stuck. I had no money, no vehicle and literally just the clothes on my back. While feverishly contemplating my situation and trying to figure out what to do with myself, I remembered this incident that had happened to me while sitting in El Paso county jail just a few years earlier ...

I had already been to county jail half a dozen times by the time I was nineteen. Each time it was the same scenario; I was usually the only white guy in the tank. Normally this would be an issue for most white boys. Remember, we're tribal by nature and being the odd man out in any situation is never fun. However, over the years of living and surviving on the streets of one of the largest Hispanic towns in America, I managed to learn the language and the people to the point where I ended up being that rare guero who spoke decent Spanish and knew enough of the big time gangbangers that I was accepted and treated like family. One afternoon in particular while sitting at one of the stainless steel tables playing chess with a well-known *narco trafficante*, the electronic iron gates opened up. To my shock, in walked this six-and-a-half-foot-tall, lanky white boy with the longest arms and the darkest tan that I have ever seen on a white person. He literally looked as though he had been lying on the beach for the last six months. His hair was bleached white with the brightest blue eyes that you could imagine. Everything about him, including the Southern California surfer accent with which he spoke, was severely out of place for the environment in which he now found himself in. Obviously, with the introduction of any new inmate to the pod, there are some preliminary "checklist" items that need to be addressed before they can settle in and make themselves comfortable. First, as always, the other gangbangers needed to know what gang someone is in. There were some current turf wars in the city of El Paso and these cholos needed to know that he was not part of any rival cliques. This was clearly a nonissue, but you never know. Secondly, we needed to know what his charges were. Apparently, there was a code of criminal ethics that was written years ago that gave drug dealers and thieves the moral superiority over rapists and sex offenders to the point where if you came to jail for a sex crime, you were open game for beatdowns and endless harassment. Again, in this particular case, it was another irrelevant issue. As this sunbaked surfer began to describe his story, I found myself completely enthralled with the details of what appeared to be one of the greatest adventure stories that I had ever heard. This California boy, maybe twenty-six years old at the time, had spent the last several years of his life working on fishing boats up in Alaska during the summer months before heading down south to the Yucatan Peninsula of Southern Mexico to live on the beach for the following eight months. This was his reoccurring annual pattern, three months on the fishing boat followed by eight months in Mexico. He shared fantastic stories of working out on the open sea near the Bering Straits just off the coast of Alaska on large seiner fishing vessels and making thousands of dollars. All of this taking place over the summer months followed by an epic journey to the southern tip of Mexico where two dollars a day would get you a hammock on the beach, all the tequila that you could drink, all the weed that you could smoke, all the psychedelic mushrooms that you could eat, beautiful girls and an epic view of some of the coolest pyramids in the western hemisphere. We were all speechless. Such a great storyteller was he that we were all there with him. At all points of his story, we were right by his side. When the fishing nets were hanging over the bow of the boat, filled with salmon and crabs, with deckhands screaming and hollering, with jellyfish falling through the net and landing on people's faces with the rain coming down hard as the sway of the waves rocked the boat back and forth, we were there. When he was hitchhiking through Chihuahua, Mexico, watching his back from the cartel gangs that patrolled those lands with assault rifles looking for any opportunities to come up at another's expense, we were there. When the sun was going down over the pyramids of tropical southern Mexico as he swayed in his two-dollar hammock with the gentle caress of the warm ocean breeze on his face, a bottle of tequila on one side and a cute senorita on the other, we were there. When he attempted to bring back a kilo of marijuana in his backpack and got popped at the international border crossing between El Paso, Texas, and Ciudad Juarez, Mexico, we were also there.

There's nothing like a good story to take your mind off the reality that you're locked up tight behind bars and have nothing really to look forward to except the stale bologna sandwich that they seem to enjoy feeding you at every meal. Needless to say, I *never* forgot that man's story and when I found myself just a few years later needing desperately to get as far away from the crime and the drugs as possible, I recalled that man's story and made a hard, fast decision that started with me calling my mom for help with a bus ticket to Seattle, Washington, to then get on a ferry boat that would take me two days journey up the Inside Passage between the shores of Canada and a string of fishing village islands before touching down safely in beautiful Ketchikan, Alaska.

I made it. I was there. The power and passion behind that man's story had influenced me to the point where I was actualizing in real time my own epic journey to go and blaze new trails and make money the honest way. Some of my fondest memories are from those reoccurring summer visits to the great state of Alaska to work that fishing industry. Some of the coolest people I have ever met in my life were friends that I had made while working and living in Alaska. I got to see orcas, humpback whales and huge pods of dolphins. I got to see the aurora borealis and wander through wild blueberry patches that went on for miles and pick some of the plumpest, juiciest blueberries from bushes that were taller than I was. I sat in drum circles, ate wild-caught salmon and halibut steaks every night and even got to sit in the captain's chair of the Scandies Rose tender boat. This was the $30 million fishing vessel that ultimately ended up sinking in the Bering Sea off Kodiak, Alaska, during a harrowing New Year's Eve ice storm that killed all but two crew members.

No, I never got to see the pyramids of Mexico. That's probably a good thing too. I most likely would have never come back. Besides, I highly doubt that all those naughty "perks" associated with living in Mexico eight months a year would be beneficial to a man who was trying to change his life for the good.

The point is when we're passionate about success and we combine that passion with a proven track record of being successful ourselves, we can motivate and inspire the people around us to dig deep and start reaching for those success stars themselves. When people see that rags-to-riches stories are possible, it gives them hope and the drive to begin learning the process of personal growth for themselves. When people see that those who had formerly walked in darkness and emptiness can pull out and have a rich, bountiful life filled with amazing experiences and true fulfillment, it awakens a dormant part of their soul to mount the courage to take the first steps needed in evolving into that person. That is why I so enjoy producing the Apex Masculinity podcast. It gives me the opportunity to share my story with so many people, both men and women, who are tired of living substandard, bottom-shelf lives. The feedback that I get is truly amazing. It inspires me to keep producing content that will inspire others to dream big and take action to becoming the man or woman who, deep down, they know that they can be.

Who are you influencing these days? You might not think that you have this power but as a man, it's a part of your DNA. We are constantly influencing and shaping the world around us by influencing and shaping the people in our immediate sphere. Your children will become both the worst and best of you. As that scale is being weighed out daily by your moment-to-moment actions, which way is it leaning? Are your kids both hearing and seeing the positive, affirming, courageous man that you can be? Or are they seeing the defeated, impulsive, fleshly man who is only concerned with himself? Even if we're just getting started with building back our lives from square one, we can still put forth a healthy, fatherly, masculine influence that helps our kids develop into grounded, successful young adults. People are always looking for a mentor or some type of positive masculine identity that resonates with them. As adults, we are still craving a fatherly influence in our lives. Even I, at forty-two years old, still find myself longing for a father, a mentor, someone who will speak positive, affirming encouragement into my life or even challenging, unsettling words of confrontation to motivate me to stop making excuses, level up and become the best version of myself. Mentors are few and far between; if you find one, count yourself a highly blessed individual. You would do well to submit yourself to that caring voice and allow it to steer, to some degree, the way to think and make choices. For years, I had to get mentorship and influence the poor man's way. Hours and hours of podcasts as I was going down the road, in whatever big rig I happened to be in, voraciously devouring every little nugget of truth and inspiration that I could get. Sometimes the trucks I would be in were older models that didn't have an aux cord insert and I'd have to just throw the hood on my hoodie up over my head and shove my phone back behind my neck, turn the volume up and listen as best as I could. I needed that mentorship. I needed that strong influence in my life. Several decades of a toxic mindset were now being replaced and transformed into a positive, courageous, self-believing mindset by allowing voices of influence to speak into my core inner man. Voices like Andrew Fereby with his Knowledge for Men podcast that inspired me to do serious analysis on my own life. Allowing me to see and believe that I was no different from any other man. If he and his guest hosts could rise up and come from damaged backgrounds and achieve great things, so could I. By allowing positive, affirming voices to challenge and inspire me to take some risk and start expecting things to work for me and not against me, I was able to see exponential growth in my own life as a man. Voices like Ryan Stewman with the Rewire podcast, a guy who sat at the same stainless steel tables, at the same penitentiary that I did, eating the same dry-ass pancakes every other day only two years earlier. A guy who got out, started from scratch and went on to become a best-selling author, success coach and multimillion-dollar business man in his industry. There's no shame in admitting that we need mentorship. In reality, it's the wiser, not the weaker, man who's willing to seek out and submit himself to being influenced. Dare I say that you yourself have even latched on to a masculine personality which resonates with you and it's caused you to begin to emulate their mannerisms, characteristics, viewpoints or ideology. I hope it's a good one. Listen, guys, a powerful tool for growth in our own lives is to allow ourselves to be influenced by the right source. For many of us that are coming into this awakening phase, we realize that we had no positive masculine role model to emulate or learn from. So what are we to do? Be fatherless, without a mentor and without a map? What is one to do in order to succeed? The better question is, what is one willing to do in order to succeed? We must be willing to seek out the positive, challenging, inspirational influence of other men who are currently walking successful, men with a proven track record of overcoming the hardships and not giving up or giving in. We must be willing to become a student of the mentorship and apply the tactics and strategies that are teased out of the mentor into our own lives. The power of influence radically changed my life. To go from a place devoid of self-confidence, self-esteem and self-worth to a place of mental strength, faith and courage isn't typical. Once a person starts down that road, they usually just continue to regress until the candle of their life eventually flickers out. I still have homies who are now in their forties or fifties who are just as stuck, broken and defeated as they were twenty-five years ago. Hopelessly lost individuals without any real chance of turning things around because rather than owning the fact that they were cheated a positive, masculine influence and finding one at whatever means necessary, they continue to chase their own tails, going around the same damn mountain, psychotically thinking that things will just one day change on their own and be better. Perpetually stuck, always wanting change but never submitting themselves to a tried and true process of personal growth and development that involves, no requires, surrendering to the truth that we need to be influenced in order to evolve and become Apex Men.

I have higher expectations of you. Don't fail me. Don't fail yourself. The most beautiful aspect of this whole endeavor is as you begin to grow and mature into a successful man by allowing yourself to be influenced by the right people, you will one day look up and find yourself being emulated by others. One day you will look up and see that the men around you are looking to you, whether it's from a distance or right up close; there will be men who your positive, self-disciplined and confidently lived life has intrigued and inspired. It's at this point that you now know that you are arriving as a man. It's at this point that you are now required to pay forward into the lives of others what was poured into you over the last several years. This is how we create exponential growth rates in changing the culture in which we live.

It's great to hit a lick and become a successful entrepreneur. It's exciting to work hard and see financial wealth and prosperity come into your life in ways that it never has before but, guys, we're talking about so much more than money. It's a full package deal. It involves becoming an emotionally grounded man who can look himself in the mirror every day and know that he's not perfect, but he's on the right path, moving in a forward direction and he can trust in his own capabilities to achieve higher levels of success in any area of life that he finds himself in. It involves becoming the husband who understands his wife and carries himself in a way that allows his wife to have all of her needs as a woman met, and I'm not just talking about the sexual ones. When's the last time that you asked your wife if she feels emotionally secure around you? When's the last time that you asked your wife if she's happy and fulfilled in her role of being your spouse. When is the last time that you asked your wife if she has any unmet needs or unfulfilled expectations in your relationship? Some of the more uncomfortable seasons of growth for me as a man were when I pinned my wife down and asked her why she was becoming disconnected and unresponsive in our marriage. If you allow your wife, as they say in the military, to "speak freely" without making excuses or vocally overpowering her, you might hear some information that can influence you to be a better man. Not a sissified, castrated tomcat, but a better man. A servant leader, one who has fulfilled the obligation to responsibly lead, nurture and develop those that are underneath his care. I don't want to be part of a one-sided relationship where, because I'm floating the bills, she should just be grateful, positive and upbeat all the time when in reality, she's quietly hurting inside or feeling oppressed, neglected or taken advantage of.

For the Apex Man, the man who wants to grow and mature at any cost, he will allow all things to become the tool of influence to help him become the better man. Whether it's the soft, glowing smile of a totally committed woman, the rough unfiltered ass-chewing that he got from his boss, the unsolicited hug of his sweet little girl or the speeding ticket that he got on his way to work. Everything in life is training him, teaching him, revealing to him where he stands, where his strengths and weaknesses are. Because he is humble, teachable and eager to learn, he will see 10x growth in his pursuit of coming out of toxicity and reforming himself as a better man.

Influence, in its natural, organic state, is able to be both positive or negative. It doesn't care which one it is. It has no moral compass, no guiding ethical law to govern its disposition. It has no burning light of integrity to illuminate its way. It just is. It just attracts whatever happens to be the core values of the man. If the man is trash, he will be attracted to and influenced by trash. If the man is lost, without any understanding of what is right or wrong, then usually whatever appeals to his flesh in the moment is what he will let himself be influenced by. I remember living in Farmington, New Mexico, back when I was seventeen years old. In the course of hanging out with different tweakers and drug addicts, I ended up meeting this guy named Steve. Steve had already been to prison multiple times. He was an old meth cook from way back when. He was probably pushing fifty years old when I met him. He had long scraggly grey hair and WHITE POWER tattooed on the back of his arms. He wasn't an arrogant ass of a man, but he carried himself with a level of confidence and stoicism that I really hadn't seen with anybody else in my circle of losers that I hung out with. Because of the striking lack of self-esteem, self-identity and self-image that I struggled with as a young man, I found myself gravitating toward this guy in a way that looking back I can clearly see was a desperate attempt to have what appeared to be a solid, confident man influence me in some way to help build a sense of identity for myself of who I was. I was lost. I was nobody. I was confused and hurting deeply in ways that I didn't even really understand. Steve was solid. I needed to be solid. Therefore, I needed to be Steve. Steve put needles in his arm. So, I put needles in my arm. Steve and I shared needles. Steve had hepatitis C ...

The power of influence is a strange thing. It all boils down to what you want to be influenced by. What appeals to you? That, my friend, is what you will hunt for. That, my friend, is what you will submit yourself to. That is what you will be influenced by.

One last story for you on the power of influence before we march on. We started this subpoint with a story about Alaska; let's end there. Shall we?

It was around about 2 a.m. on a Saturday night. Kito's Cave was the name of the drinking establishment that all of us transient cannery rats would get soused at. We had gotten the weekend off from the salmon cannery that half the town seemed to be employed by. So naturally, my buddy Dirty Dave and I were enjoying the free time playing pool and harassing the other patrons while downing overpriced microbrews. Normally, from June 1 until about the second week of September, the fishing industry is so busy that it doesn't afford even the slightest bit of break or rest to spend even a day, let alone an entire weekend, getting smashed at the local pub. The only other bar in the small fishing village of Petersburg, Alaska, was a quiet little place called the Harbor Bar. There was never any real excitement at the Harbor Bar. The local police chief liked to drink there on occasion, so over the years it became known as the "locals" bar while all the migrant workers who were only there for the fishing season would end up at Kito's Cave. Much like any West Coast dive bar, there were pool tables, live bands, hot waitresses and lots of drunk fishermen. The only real difference between me and the man that I was in the preceding paragraph is that I was two years older and employed. I was certainly just as lost and undoubtedly just as insecure, still impressionable and wanting desperately to be influenced by someone still, in hopes of developing some sense of personal identity.

Dirty Dave was now that man. Slightly older, cocky as any, and certainly a very self-assured young man. He was six feet two, built like a tank and, yes, there was a reason we called him Dirty Dave. He always seemed to be focused on one thing. Yup.

As the bartender was bellowing out for last call, Dave leaned in real close over the pool table and, in a hushed grin, informed me that he had secured a twenty-dollar sack of cocaine from this Mexican dude named El Vampiro and thought it would be a great idea if we purchased a fifth of vodka before the bar closed and then strolled down to the docks to steal a boat and sail out to Sockeye Island. Obviously, from my perspective, this seemed a downright fantastic idea seeing as how I hadn't used any hard drugs since I left the lower forty-eight states for my current Alaska adventure.

As we approached the docks and the countless numbers of boats both small and great that littered the wooden piers along the shoreline, ol' Dirty Dave surprised me by getting cold feet. In a last-minute moment of reflection, he came to the conclusion that what we were doing was a bad idea because "If we stole one with a motor, it would be considered theft of a motor vehicle if we happened to get caught." So, in his vodka-induced wisdom, he suggested that we steal a canoe because "It didn't have a motor." Theft of a motor vehicle was a Class C felony in the state of Alaska. Petty theft of personal property was only a misdemeanor. So, trusting in the well-rounded and exhaustive legal education that Dirty Dave seemed so thoroughly versed in, we popped cork, weighed anchor and set sail.

Navigating out of the harbor was as eventful as you might expect for two highly intoxicated individuals who had about as much common sense as they did fine motor skills. It was one of those staggering expeditions where we kept banging our canoe off every other boat in the harbor before loudly whispering that the other person needed to shut the hell up and be quiet, followed by hilarious laughter because the other guy wouldn't shut the heck up and be quiet. You know what I'm talking about? We finally got far enough away from the harbormaster to where it didn't really matter anymore if we were quiet and that's when we decided to really cut loose and carry on like the swashbuckling idiots that we were currently in character for. As we sailed the midnight seas snorting lines of coke and chasing it down with some of the cheapest, gut rot, bottom-shelf vodka that you could buy, we sang pirate songs and told epic tales about how badass we were. Both of us in T-shirts and jeans that smelled like a salmon cannery as we rowed and drank and snorted on our clandestine adventure across the three-mile expanse of open ocean that would lead us out to Sockeye Island for whatever purpose; to this day, I still have no clue but we were committed and not to be deterred.

Funny thing is the ocean itself is always on the move. For those who don't know, the tide is always somewhere in its cyclical process of either coming in or going out. For a short portion of the day, the tide will sit still but not for very long as the moon and its gravitational pull begin their seductive influence on the water. As we started our epic journey, it just so happened to be that time of the night where the tide was standing still. There was a calmness on the water that allowed my tank of a friend to make real, measurable headway with every stroke of the oars. As we pressed further into the vastness of the open sea, we started noticing that the canoe that we were in was a bit rundown. Had we done a good pre-trip inspection on our equipment, we might have noticed a few issues of concern. But, who has time for that? We were on a mission, damn it.

After a few hours had passed, the tide decided that it was going to reverse itself and start heading out, away from the shore. Hallelujah! Whatever pace we had been making was now dwarfed in comparison as every stroke of the oars combined with the outward pull of the tide now propelled us speedily toward our destination. We celebrated with a final chug on the bottle and the last two lines of coke from the paper pouch it had been so neatly packaged in for distribution.

After another heartfelt chorus of "Yo ho, yo ho, a pirate's life for me," we began to notice the weather shift and shift it did. Within just a few minutes, it seemed as though the clouds had rolled in from nowhere, completely shrouding the moonlight, leaving us navigationally stranded by blindness. We couldn't see the shoreline; we couldn't make out the silhouette of Sockeye Island. We could barely see each other. We just sat there, in the darkness, uncertain of how to proceed. Someone decided that it might be a good idea to just start paddling back in the direction that we assumed the harbor was in. That's when the rain started to fall. In Southeast Alaska, the rain can fall anywhere from up to twenty-six days a month in some cases. Whether it's a torrential downpour, a slow and miserable dribble or the partly frozen sleeting shit that was now falling on our hungover, T-shirted, moron of the year award-winning asses, it's guaranteed to hit you out of nowhere when you least expect it and when it hurts you the most. Ask any fisherman. Damn. We were in bad shape.

After another short burst of rowing like a bat out of hell in what we prayed was the right direction, one of the O-rings that the oars slide through for swiveled rowing ended up breaking out of the wooden frame of the canoe.

Really? Like, are you serious? We were, as they say, "dead in the water." Things were escalating from bad to worse at a rapid pace. By this time, the rain had given way to dense fog just as the sun had begun to rise up out from behind the peaks of Petersburg Mountain. We were frozen, shivering, and hungover with a splitting headache from that gut-rot bottom-shelf vodka. By now, the coke had worn off and there was nothing adventurous nor fun about our current situation. We couldn't see but twenty feet around us in any given direction; that's when the humpback whale breached topside next to our boat. Yup. No joke. No hallucinations. No embellishment for ratings. As if being sucked out to sea by the tide wasn't enough, we had to endure the sheer terror of a massive ocean-dwelling creature pulling up alongside our boat to investigate our sad, disconcerting plight. As you can imagine, in the obscurity of the fog, not being sure right away with what I was seeing, every *Jaws* movie that I've ever watched flooded through my mind as this docile and truly harmless ocean-dwelling, toothless, plankton-eating mammal popped in on us for a curious peek at what we might have been doing so far out in these parts in such a tiny little bucket of a craft. It was so close to us that I could see its starboard-side eye looking right at us. In my partially drunken state of mind, I could have sworn that the look in its eye was one more of empathy and sympathy than anything remotely angered, dangerous or nefarious. Almost like the look of a frustrated grandmother looking down the bridge of her nose through raised glasses at two mischievous boys who definitely needed a good whooping for their behavior but were too scared and pathetic in the moment to add any increase in trauma for their stupid mistake. A moment later, it expelled its blowhole full of water that, thanks to the wind, sprayed all over us and added another two inches of water to the floor line of our rain-filled skiff before submerging itself out of sight forever. I made the decision to bequeath all my last possessions to Dave just in case I didn't make it out alive. I think I had thirty-five cents and a cigarette lighter to my name. I whimperingly handed it all over, telling Dave through chattering, shivering teeth, "I love you, buddy; you should have these things. I'm going to lie down and die now." At which point I lay down in the boat, in two inches of water, curled up in the fetal position, waiting for the boat to capsize, sink or be eaten. I couldn't tell if Dave was laughing or crying at this point; he had been so positive thus far. The swiveled O-ring tearing free from the wood was the final straw of hope being wrenched from his hands. All of that strength would no longer be serving us as we continued to bob through the briny surf like a chunk of doomed driftwood, aimlessly coursing our way toward the next port of land, which at this point I believed would either be the Philippines or Korea. This sucked. How did this happen? Who did this to me?

As the good Lord would have it, we ended up not having dinner in Singapore that evening, nor were we eaten by a giant squid. To our ecstatic surprise, through a break in the fog, we noticed a seiner fishing vessel passing by on its way back to port and with desperate, flailing arms and shivering, whimpering voices, we managed to flag the captain down and get towed back to the harbor where guess who was anxiously anticipating our arrival? Yup. The harbormaster and the local law enforcement authorities with shiny bracelets in hand were eagerly waiting to chauffeur our happy, hungover asses down to the local hoosegow.

As we reached the docks, the harbormaster smirkingly greeted Dave. "Top o' the morning to you, captain," he said. No response. With heads down in shame and a large crowd now gathering to see what all the action was about, we were loaded into the paddy wagon and hauled up the hillside to the local hospital where this sad, comical yet absolutely verifiable story about influence comes to an end. The crowning jewel of the adventure of a lifetime ended with a cold glass thermometer to the keister to check for hypothermia before being locked behind bars, thus becoming a "no call, no show" for work that following morning. After a scathing rebuke from the local judge and a hellacious fine was imposed, we were allowed to return to the normalcy of life to wallow in our mired reputations and finish working the salmon season.

The power of influence is quietly at work every day. Every moment we are either influencing others or being influenced. Make sure you're influencing people in a direction that serves their greater good. Also, make damn sure that no one is influencing you in a direction that's going to take you further than you want to go, keep you longer than you want to stay, and cost you more than you want to pay. I'd hate for anyone else to get the glass thermometer. I don't care how small it is; it always hurts when it's nonconsensual.

11. Self-aware people are always mindful of how they are treating others. Let's be honest. We've all most likely had the unfortunate experience of meeting that one self-absorbed, narcissistic ass of a man who only condescends to entertain a relationship or a conversation with someone so that he can determine how he's going to capitalize on or manipulate that person to his support his own inflated ego or accomplish his own selfish ambitions. You know, that one guy who constantly talks over people and doesn't care to listen as others speak because he's too busy drafting his next superior response to their obviously inferior intellect. The problem with people like this is that they are often so full of themselves that they are completely oblivious to the distasteful way in which they treat other people. They are mired in self-deception, believing themselves to be respected and revered by many when, in fact, they are despised and loathed by all who wander across their egocentric path. These are the psychic vampires that excel in the art of emotionally draining weak-minded and naïve people who haven't yet gotten hip to the idea that ugly people exist out there that care for no one but themselves. These are the trolls that take advantage of the simple minded, using manipulation tactics to make other people feel guilty for not serving their needs and wants on demand. The scariest aspect of these parasites

is that oftentimes they are completely unaware that they are even behaving this way. On the few times in life when someone points out their manipulative, selfish behavior, they will usually run from the conversation or blame the other person rather than own their negativity and try to work on fixing it.

On the other hand, self-aware people, in most cases, can walk away from any interaction with someone and know that they handled that person with the utmost dignity and respect. Even if they had to be stern or confrontational. Learning to be mindful in the moment-to-moment personal interactions spares us the work of having to go back and analyze those previous interactions to make sure we emanated a positive, respectful tone or made that person feel as though their input was as important to us as we would like our input to be to them.

Being able to make someone feel safe and respected allows them to put their guard down, giving you access to another layer of depth inside the true person. They now no longer are suspicious of your next attack; they now no longer have to hold a defensive posture against you as they wait for your next aggressive, interrogative barrage of demeaning accusations against their character. This is nothing more than your own self-righteous insecurity attempting to expose every flaw or weakness or bad decision that you believe to be true of them to make yourself feel superior. This is what causes people to put guards up. This is what causes people to be impersonal, superficial and vague in their interactions with others.

Can you blame them? They've learned over the years not to give you any ammunition against them. So they choose to stay shallow and measured in their interactions with you. You get only surface-level interactions with them because they've learned that your agenda is to tear down others in order to elevate yourself. We're hard enough on ourselves without having to put up with someone else scavenging for every predatorial opportunity to work us over in a conversation or take a manipulative, advantageous position against us in order to keep us in a box that their insecure, uncaring mind can control.

PRINCIPLE 3:

THE LEGACY PRINCIPLE

I never saw it coming. It was just after five on a foggy South Texas morning. The sky was dense with clouds, shrouding the moonlight and providing a blanket of darkness that settled over the wet morning. The fog held complete dominion over the landscape, challenged only by the foreboding reddish glow of the traffic light at which I now sat. The lights held their own, but barely. Their desperate attempt to exercise authority and visibility over the hundred yards of turf that they had been commissioned to alert and protect was diminishing by the moment. Idling at the intersection in my little white Nissan, staring so intently at the glowing crimson lantern hanging above, I almost didn't even notice the subtle shift to green. I eased into the throttle ...

BAM! The semi hit me broadside. As a professional truck driver myself, I routinely look first. As we were taught in school, left, right, then left again. Not today. My mind, under the stress of a myriad of recent personal failures and current problems, coupled with the fatigue of too many early morning commutes, had me in my own fog mentally. Distracted by the current state of affairs not only in our economy but in my own life, living in an RV with my wife and three kids, hauling gravel around San Antonio, making just enough to be broke and barely surviving, contemplating all the bad choices and tragic setbacks over the last few years, I pulled through the intersection, left-hand blinker of the tiny Versa politely advising the world that we now had the right of way before being effortlessly lifted off the ground by the homicidal kiss of a belly dump doing seventy miles an hour fully loaded at forty tons trying to "make the light."

I was now liberated from my fog. Everything from the windshield out to the front license plate was gone. The shattered glass, fragments of copper, nuts, bolts and wire were like a drunken blast of confetti on New Year's Eve. Even the transmission was completely gone. Which, of course, prevented me from being able to put the vehicle in park and allowing the doors to automatically unlock so I could climb out. I was, for the moment, trapped. In that instant, I gained clarity on two things that for me had been rumors only up to that point. One, it truly doesn't hurt near as bad if you don't see it coming and two, sodium azide and potassium nitrate do indeed instantaneously combine to form nitrogen gas, filing up deployed airbags in your vehicle located in places you would never have even imagined that they are installed.

Oddly enough, the excitement wasn't quite finished that morning. There was an ample string of vehicles behind my assailant that stopped to render aid. An elderly African American couple was first on the scene. I've never been more impressed by the phenomenon of super-strength caused by adrenaline rushing through the human body that takes place during moments of catastrophic excitement. There was no earthy way that she should have been able, with her feeble, arthritic frame, to pick up, let alone hurl, a boulder of that size through the back window of my car, allowing me a passage of escape.

In my bewilderment, I inaccurately mistook the smell of nitrogen gas being released from the deflating airbags as smoke, leading me to believe that my car was on fire. I didn't even notice the arms of the young Hispanic man on his way to work that morning reach in through the crater that had once been my window and bear hug me out through the shattered gaping void setting my feet firmly on safe, solid asphalt. There was a silent moment where we just stared at each other. I reached out, arms wide open, grateful for the assistance. He hugged me back without any awkwardness like two cousins who hadn't seen each other in over a decade.

At this point, I peeked back through the fractured glass to make sure my lifeless corpse wasn't slumped over the steering wheel before my disembodied spirit was whisked off into a shimmering glow of warm light to engage in whatever activities await all who embark on that second half of the eternal bus ride.

Ridiculous as it may seem, my morning brush with the Reaper wasn't quite through. Huddled around the devastated wreckage that was once my car, traffic stopped in all directions, people on their phones dialing 911, muttering and chattering in astonishment about "how they totally expected to see a dead body," and "how they couldn't believe that truck driver tried to just drive off," a young lady on her way to work coming from the opposite direction decided to confirm the answer to another age-old physics problem. Foggy conditions x limited visibility + four bald tires to the power of wet asphalt squared always equals ... misfortune.

As she locked the brakes up she jerked the steering wheel hard to avoid slamming her car into all the vehicles halted in that space that shouldn't have been there but were cloaked from visibility by that unnaturally compressed fog sending her on a spiraling path through the intersection directed straight toward myself, my first responders and what was left of my car. Another miracle was bestowed on the children of men that morning as her paint-faded '86 Lincoln Town Car was stopped drifting sideways only inches from our gathering. People were literally screaming and diving face-first out of the way to avoid being plowed over by this tank of a vehicle barreling toward them sideways, at least forty miles an hour.

I felt so bad for this young girl, maybe seventeen. Nineteen at most, as the infuriated crowd did not restrain themselves from expressing in no uncertain terms their sore displeasure at her obvious inability to control her vehicle ... or the laws of physics and momentum for that matter. It was the most surreal experience I have ever had.

The flashlight in my eyes checking for evidence of concussion snapped me back to focus. My street-side examination by the paramedic, coupled with the bright flashing lights of the state police, having now placed an authoritative sense of order over the situation, caused me to finally relax a bit. My neck was on fire.

"Do you need to go to the hospital, sir?"

"I-I don't know," was my stammered response. "Sir, I highly advise you to go to the hospital for X-rays." "Yes, of course," I replied. I was confused, in shock and basically being led to whatever next right decision was being recommended for me.

My ambulance ride to Guadalupe Regional Medical Center included a fancy white neck brace and a first-time opportunity to lie down on a gurney and ride stylishly in the back of an EMS transport. Cognizant and in stable condition, we opted for strobe lights only, sparing the surrounding residential communities of the obnoxious sirens that seek only to remind all who hear them that shit happens quick and tomorrow isn't promised to anyone.

Lying on the gurney, I had a somber introspection that saddened me to my core. What if that had been the one? That fateful day that eventually awaits all of us. That final punch of the time clock of life that closes our eyes for the last time and robs everyone that you know and love of your existence, leaving only memories, photos and an experience of grief that

I think most people would agree is the most painful to accept and difficult to heal from. Death.

How would my family survive without me? No possessions of value, no money in the bank, not even life insurance to assist in the cost associated with my burial. Worse yet, how would I be remembered? What had I accomplished in life? I certainly wasn't the worst person that I knew, but I absolutely wasn't the best version of myself by a long shot either.

Gentlemen, I ask you, what is legacy? How is it built? Is it even important and why?

As stated earlier, I'm not a deep thinker on all topics; I live a pretty simple life, but when stumped by something, I feel the need to educate myself. So, I began a project of self-analysis that took me deeper into myself than I've ever cared or dared to go. I wasn't impressed with myself or with much of what I had accomplished up to that point. As I began to reflect over the thirty-five-year journey that had led me to become the man who I then was, I kept seeing patterns, reoccurring themes. I had developed an uncanny knack for self-sabotage, I didn't ever play the long game, I seldom finished what I started, I was pleasure-driven and experience-driven rather than integrity-driven and accomplishment-driven. Most importantly, I learned that over the last three decades, I had developed a self-limiting belief system that had me literally locked out of ever hoping to live a truly rewarding, fulfilling and successful life.

If I've learned anything over the last several years of studying psychology, I can unequivocally guarantee you that, whether consciously or subconsciously, we will always behave and make choices in accordance with what we believe about ourselves to be true. You will live how you see yourself to be. Your level of success in any area of life will seldom exceed your level of personal belief about yourself in that role. If you see yourself as a loser and believe that you're a loser ... then you will be one. Even if you desperately don't want to be one. If your subconscious mind believes you to be substandard, then it freaks out when you try to be anything but substandard. The act of you attempting to be successful doesn't synch with the several decades worth of toxic, substandard and negative programming that your conscious and subconscious mind have matured into being. Therefore, usually in a frantic attempt to simply cause our lives to match what we believe, you and I will usually do something self-sabotaging to bring ourselves back to the level of success and "normality" that we're accustomed to. Which often is substandard.

Almost like a mind-possessing parasite (your subconscious) that takes complete control of its host (your behavior), you will watch in horror as you begin to make toxic decisions and, in the process, commit self-destructive behaviors that will always bring you right back to the level of success that you believe you are allowed to have. You will become a compliant coconspirator with your own subconscious in the crime of perpetual self-sabotage. In clinical psychology, this behavior is diagnosed as cognitive dissonance.

Cognitive dissonance is simply defined as the state of having inconsistent thoughts, beliefs or attitudes, especially as relating to behavioral decisions and attitude change. This is why some of us feel like frauds when we start becoming successful. It's called impostor syndrome. As we start becoming less self-destructive and more successful in life, there is a part of us, embedded deep within our subconscious mind, that knows where we've been; it knows what we've done and, as a result, it has formulated a resolute and unyielding opinion that we do not qualify for or deserve success. In many cases, it's the negative, demeaning voice inside our own head that was planted there several decades ago by a critical, condemning parent coupled with the memory of every failure that we've experienced along the way. This unhealthy and very real disorder can become so mentally loud and pressing that a person isn't able to find peace in success. After they've had enough of the emotional and psychological chaos that's taking place in their own head, they will eventually just do something stupid to quickly get it over with so that they can go back to being what they've always been. So that they can go back to being what that voice inside their head tells them that they are. So that they can once again live in alignment with what their subconscious believes is acceptable for them. This is the contented place of quiet desperation. It's the dirty little security blanket that should have been tossed in the garbage long ago but it gives them comfort because they're used to it.

Oddly enough, the mind gets accustomed to experiencing life in a certain way. An even more bizarre notion is the idea that it doesn't like change. Whether it's positive or negative, our minds simply want consistency. Consistency is predictable. Consistency is safe. Safe and predictable is staying alive.

Listen close, my friend; it doesn't matter what types of opportunities might happen along your way in life. If you're lucky enough to get a degree, learn a trade or stumble across some other type of business opportunity, none of those things will make you successful. Even the best, once-in-a-lifetime type opportunities will eventually come crashing down around your ankles as long as that self-sabotaging voice and that toxic belief system still exists inside of you.

Things may start out well enough but it won't be long before that monster in you ruins that financial opportunity or that great relationship with that awesome person who could have been the "one."

We must learn to convince ourselves that we deserve better and are capable of achieving and maintaining increasing levels of success in our lives. For me, it was raw, blunt honesty that helped to reform the neuro-programming. In addition to just learning about myself and practicing the art of making better, thoughtful choices, I also implemented an honest self-diagnosis along the way. Rather than lie and say to myself that I was the best husband or the best father, I would just be honest and say "I've got a lot to learn but I'm on the path, learning more and becoming more in this area every day." This "room to grow" type mentality not only helped me recover faster from the failures that I committed along the way but it empowered and reminded me that there's a greater cause to get up and fight for every day.

If you're one of those unfortunate, cynical people in life who have adopted the mantra of "something's wrong with everything all of the time," then you're really going to struggle to gain the necessary momentum and traction that's so desperately needed, especially in the beginning to get the ship of your life off of the ground and headed in the right direction. We must learn to change the story that we're telling ourselves. That is termed self-induced neurolinguistic programming. As you and I begin to profess a better story for ourselves, we can truly begin to create a mindset of self-confidence and a healthy belief system about the actual possibilities of how all of this can turn out.

Everyone loves a great underdog story of how someone rose up from the ashes of hell and darkness with what appeared to be a hopeless situation and, through self-determination and grace, went on to achieve great things. It's a beautiful process. One that many will start but few will ever finish because it can be severely painful at times. Yet, therein lies the beauty of the evolution.

The journey of learning how to reform and excel in any area of life should be treasured and revered just as much as the arrival and attainment of that goal. If you just woke up one morning and every area of your life went from broken, toxic and substandard to blameless, flawless and perfect, you wouldn't appreciate what you had become. You would truly be cheated of the glory, the honor and the self-satisfaction that's associated with overcoming so many obstacles and maturing into the Apex Man.

Where the cognitive dissonance or inconsistency in our thoughts and belief systems stems from is the idea that even though there's a very real part of us that's comfortable staying the way we've always been, there's also a very real part of ourselves that is dissatisfied with the idea of staying the same because it knows that we were made and destined for more. We were made for higher living. We were designed for better results and a better, more fulfilling quality of life.

This dichotomy of belief is why we feel like fraudulent and unfulfilled men when we're stuck in a place of unsuccess. Due to the gnawing fact that at our core level, in a place separate from our subconscious, we know that we are living beneath our means and capabilities. We know that immense levels of maturity, wisdom, self-control and success are attainable if we'll just start, stay faithful to the process and never give up no matter what comes our way.

I'm sure you can imagine how chaotic, stressed, dissatisfied and unsettled one would be in their mind from day to day or even moment to moment trying to reconcile or make sense of these two competing voices or ideologies that live in the same space but are diametrically opposed to each other in every way. As men, this is what we become in life. We've grown up in unhealthy environments that have shaped, over the years of childhood and adolescence, a toxic and cynical mindset that limits and affects to varying degrees our levels of self-confidence, self-worth, self-image, self-respect and self-esteem. Yet, by trial and error, just over the natural course of time, we have also gained a sizable set of life experiences where we have succeeded and achieved goals that we have set for ourselves. There's the voice of criticism and doubt screaming at us upstairs, but there's also a voice, from our center, reminding us of times along the journey where we dug deep and won some limited but very real victories in life. Again, self-doubt screaming from upstairs and courage challenging us from our core.

The unfortunate irony is these conflicting viewpoints don't cancel each other out. Instead, they constantly fight each other for ownership and dominion of your perspective on how you see yourself as a man. These two opposing viewpoints are emboldened and empowered at different seasons in life based on a myriad of different yet very relatable circumstances, like are we plateauing in life, which can cause idleness and irritability for those of us who are more conquest-driven. Or, are we in a season where unexpected, back-to-back tragedies are taking place. Seasons of tribulation befall everyone but the mind has a way of convincing us that unexpected setbacks only happen to us. If we're not careful, this line of thinking can take you to a dark place and keep you there longer than you want to stay, costing you time. I promise you, everyone in life deals with adversity. Even the apex people of the world have to deal with unexpected misfortunate circumstances from time to time. Rest assured, these tougher seasons in life are never fun but if we maintain the right perspective, they can usually result in some of our greatest seasons of growth and maturity as men. Having a positive attitude during these times is key in assisting our destined-self voice to sing louder than our doubting-self voice. Either way, I promise you this, trying times are not the result of some diabolical plan in which the universe hates only you and is systematically trying to kill you.

In addition, the amount of sleep that we get, or lack thereof, can have a serious impact on which of these two perspectives will rule the day. Getting adequate sleep plays a huge factor in our ability to think clearly, have better self-control and better overall governance of our emotions. I can't count the times in my life where exhaustion was the primary factor in making a very impulsive, very destructive decision that quite honestly set me back two steps rather than propels me forward. We need to value our rest and make sure that we're recharging the machine. We don't need to get it all done in a day; that's what tomorrow is for. We certainly don't need to be getting up early for work in the morning and then staying up late carousing all night getting drunk or staying glued to a screen playing video games or binge-watching the latest season of *The Walking Dead*. Living like that night after night catches up with you. It slows you down. It steals your drive and ambition to achieve a higher, rewarding, more fulfilling life. When we live that way, we'll notice ourselves starting to settle rather than strive. We'll notice ourselves beginning to be lulled into a quiet, pacified slumber of sedated contentment. Or maybe you won't notice it happening at all ...

Another important factor in maintaining a positive, healthy perspective from day to day is the quality of your nutritional intake. This will also have a tremendous impact on your perception of yourself and your ability to stay grounded and focused on the idea that you can win in life. Our minds and our bodies are the tools that are given to us to achieve and enjoy the legacy that we choose to build for ourselves. When we treat our machine like garbage, garbage is what it will produce. It blows my mind to think that something as simple as staying well hydrated and getting a reasonable amount of vitamins and minerals on a daily basis can 10x the amount of success that we attain in life. Living healthy creates the mental focus and the clarity of mind to draft in our brains a success blueprint that's specific to our personal situation in life. One that we can begin to live out and see manifest in real time. Being healthy gives us a sound and solid mind that can adjust, adapt and improvise quickly as and if the need ever arises. Rather than walking in a moronic fog of uncertainty because our brain is nutritionally deficient and just letting life happen to us, we can draft, implement and strive toward our goals and ambitions as men.

One of the leading causes of disease is having a lowered immune system. Our immune systems are strengthened through vitamins and minerals that our bodies were designed to convert and use for a healthy existence. Staying hydrated allows for those vitamins and minerals to have the adequate fluid that your body needs to pass those nutrients to every section of your body. It doesn't even need to be this epic, over-the-top reformation of your entire life where you wake up one day and become this vegan, paleo, ketogenic, non-carb, no-fat, sugar-free Atkins-friendly guy with a man bun, a yoga mat, smelling like you swam across a river of patchouli oil before smoking a fatty laced with nag champa and sandalwood. You don't have to spend the rest of your life eating spirulina and equitably sourced, fair-traded cage-free chicken feathers to create a noticeable, positive change in your overall health.

For me, it's as simple as a green smoothie in the morning made with kale, spinach and avocado for maximum absorption, followed by a multivitamin, a thousand milligrams of vitamin C and five thousand milligrams of vitamin D. I drink excessive amounts of water because for me dehydration converts to fatigue, which ultimately converts to being stagnant and undriven.

I still have cream and sugar in my coffee, I still eat a lot of what you would call typical American dishes but I eat more vegetables, I supplement my subpar American diet with vitamins and fiber-rich foliage and I live mindful, from day to day, of the fact that nutrition, hydration and adequate sleep are critical components to my overall success and healthy frame of mind. These are the precursor elements that are essential in building and maintaining a productive, fulfilling legacy.

Now that we've established the importance of having a healthy mind and body as the foundation stone on which we will build our legacy, let's now look at the reasons why building that epic legacy is so important

As we move on to the actual process of building a legacy, one must first understand why our legacy is not only important but that it's actually the crowning jewel of our entire life.

Webster's dictionary defines legacy as a gift or possession bestowed on another from a predecessor at will. At will simply meaning at the disclosure of the legal documents that contain the contents of your last wishes after you pass away. Not a very exciting definition when one considers the way the term legacy is tossed about today. As though it were some epic achievement that you acquire in your relentless pursuit of success, like some crown jewel that once acquired can be relished on and doted over by the legatee for soaring to a certain altitude of prosperity or fame in life. In short, gentlemen, legacy is nothing more than what you will be remembered by, and as, after your departure from this temporary dwelling place that we call earth. Legacy can never be appreciated by the man. Only the process of building an epic legacy may be appreciated and enjoyed. For your legacy develops and gains, whether negative or positive, up until your last whispered breath.

Our legacy is something we will never hold personally in our own hands. In fact, it is something that will never be discussed, or even mused over, until we step into the afterlife, at which point it will matter very little to you. We may hold and cherish another's legacy and enjoy, as it were, contemplating and discussing the legendary achievements of another person's triumphs and conquests. But you and I, by rule, and the very definition of legacy, are not allowed to hold our own. Our only engagement, our only enjoyment, or regret in the architecture of building a personal legacy is so that others may one day hold, hopefully praise, and benefit from the lifelong endeavors that you and I are building today. Every choice to take positive action and create, or take negative action that tears down and destroys, will determine the day-to-day growth rate and quality of the reputation and legacy that we are building. Even when being passive and taking no action, you and I are quietly building our legacy.

A better definition of legacy, one that I believe boils it all down, is to see our legacy as a four-legged table that will either fatten or malnourish all who sit thereby. The table is your life. The table is supported by four legs. Personal legacy development is defined in four ways: (1) legacy is what you acquire, (2) legacy is what you accomplish, (3) legacy is who you become, and (4) legacy is who you influence.

Let's take a look in detail at each of the four attributes of building a legacy. The first, and in my opinion, the least important of the four but important enough that it deserves discussion, is what you acquire. Legacy involves what you acquire in life. Not from a place of greed but from a place of being able to accumulate wealth and possessions to experience and provide a richer quality of life. Not only for yourself but for your loved ones, for the people who are depending on you to give them your very best. Albert Einstein was indeed correct in his equation that time is money. The more money that we have, the less we will need to work. The less we need to work, the more time we will have to the activities that are important to us, and to the people who are equally important to us. Countless numbers of men in this country, every day, after slaving away for several decades of their life to make someone else rich, step into the afterlife, leaving nothing of perpetual value for their families. They leave behind them nothing except fleeting memories that fade with the passing of time and an $11,000 burial fee that most families will end up going into debt to take care of. For many, there exists a quiet indifference in building a solid, enduring financial portfolio that will not only outlive the man but will outlive the needs that exist after the man is gone. I know it may sound judgmental. That's not the angle I want to portray in my perspective on the matter. Many a man truly does the best that he can with what he has. That will always be in itself a commendable attribute. However, we can't deny the cold reality that many more a man is perfectly capable of building himself a better quality of life and leaving for others a better legacy. Whether it's laziness, complacency or ignorance of the strategies that exist to build, too many men are simply choosing to roll the dice instead of rising to the challenge of building a personal legacy.

I don't want to live my life in a way where, when I finally pass on, my passing is a tremendous burden toward the people who I'm obligated to make damn sure are set up and equipped to carry on. As a family man, it no longer is about you. It's about them. Can you and I, in this self-absorbed, self-centered culture, adopt for ourselves a mindset that truly believes that the better man is always the one who lived his life for others, who made wiser, more disciplined choices not only for his own benefit but for the betterment and overall success of those around him. Remember this, my friend, the man who is *poured out* into others, is himself *fulfilled*. The man who is *spent* for the wellness of others is truly *saved*. The man who *lays down* his life for others, he himself, *triumphs* over all.

What does your gut tell you? How do you see the matter? Would you not agree that it's commendable and respectable, as men, for us to acquire not only character and integrity on our journey through life but wealth and possessions for our family to be able to enjoy? The love of money is truly the root of all evil but before you think of me as greedy, shallow, or materialistic in my pursuit to be wealthy, we should consider what wealth acquisition allows for. Does the prospect of owning a home with a plot of land that's yours, that provides a safe and healthy place for your kids to grow up, explore and comfortably enjoy their childhood experience seem shallow? As a side note, as I'm writing this very chapter, my wife and I just sold a home for $201,000 that we bought two years ago in Colorado. We bought it for $160,000. Nothing overwhelmingly amazing but we netted $41,000 of passive investment money by investing in a property and selling at the right time. You can't do things like that when you're stuck in low-income housing or living in a beat-down crack house of a trailer that's losing value by the day. I can say that without feeling arrogant or condescending because I've experienced both of those living situations and I can tell you, my friend, there's truly a better way.

Does being able to take your kids and sign them up for sporting events seem materialistic? We signed my son up for basketball this year and the life experiences that he gained in the process were invaluable. He learned that he's capable of being a valuable team member whose contributions toward the greater good were appreciated. He learned how to lose gracefully. He learned how to defend his space against another young man. He learned that practice increases the likelihood of success. He learned that risk can sometimes bring great reward. These are all lessons that will assist him in excelling further in his own journey as a man. Yet, it wasn't free to buy uniforms, basketball shoes, sign-up fees or gas money to travel to some of these games. It may seem like a trivial and relatively small example but you'd be surprised to know how many families there are in America that simply can't afford the costs associated with something like this.

The goal is always for the greater good of your family. A simple way to do that is to be wise with what you have and make plans to progressively increase your profitability as you go. It instills a quiet satisfaction knowing that you did your best to raise them right, provide for them the best life experience possible and to position them well in the event of your unexpected loss.

I don't want my passing to be the final burden that I place on my loved ones. Not wanting to be the harbinger of doom, but as a gentle reminder, that final day is coming for all of us. It's the one event that none of us can escape. All of us will pass from this life into the next. What did you build? What did you leave for them? How much easier or difficult will it be for them at that time because of the choices that you made or didn't make today. As stated earlier, most families will go into debt as they finance funerals and burials for their loved ones. Imagine that for a moment, if you will, eighteen months after you're dead and gone, your lovely wife is still trying to scrape together the $400-a-month payment to the funeral home or to the crematory where they had to incinerate you because they couldn't afford to purchase a proper burial for you. Here she is, already laden with a tremendous burden of grief at your passing combined with all the hard work of trying to keep your children emotionally in check as they learn to adjust and cope with your untimely demise and now every month, instead of working toward healing from the pain of your loss, your wife gets a monthly reminder via a bill statement, not only of your passing but of the taxing expense in which you so abruptly left. I don't want that. You don't want that.

I have three daughters that I love and care for very much, who I would love to streamline weddings for one day when they're ready, without having to max out credit cards and go into debt to do so. They deserve to be blessed like that and I deserve the privilege of being able to provide that experience for them. It's not something that I'll be able to do though if I'm living paycheck to paycheck, drinking or smoking away every extra dollar that I have. It will forever be an unattainable dream if I'm not demonstrating wisdom in my finances by being self-disciplined in how I manage, save and invest my money.

I would love to be able to travel overseas and take my kids with me, allowing them to experience other cultures that will ultimately enrich them as human beings. Obviously, this is not an essential experience for a child in order for them to grow up and be grounded and solid in how they carry themselves as an adult, but it would undoubtedly be a highly rewarding event for them to enjoy. Moments like this speak volumes to children. Especially as it relates to what they see and believe are possibilities for themselves. If you keep them stuck in poverty their entire lives, then they will grow up expecting and settling into poverty for themselves. Embracing poverty and meager living will be their natural default position on what they expect and deserve for themselves. I'm not suggesting that we spoil our children by catering to every whimsical desire that they have. I am, however, suggesting that you show them in real time, a life that teaches them that the possibilities are limitless in what they can experience and responsibly enjoy in life if they work hard, be wise and value themselves.

I would love to be able to purchase safety-rated, high-quality vehicles for my children when they're ready to start driving.

I would love to be able to purchase time and tenure at college for them so that they can learn a trade so that, when they step out into the world ready to build their own legacy, they're head and shoulders above most of the labor force. It's fierce and competitive out there. If there's anything that I can do as a father to ensure their success, then I should be committed to try and do that.

Much of the world lives in a place of poverty. But the dirty little secret, guys, is that they don't have to. It's about buckling down, being disciplined, and not living for experiences and pleasures from day to day. That can come later. There must be discipline and restraint on the front side to build the capital that's necessary to enjoy living like that. It involves restraining oneself and saving; it's about making investments that will turn a dollar in the future. It's about being patient and letting your money work for you. What you acquire, both possessions and finances in life, is an essential part of building a solid, respectable legacy.

The next aspect of a man's legacy, or what we would call the next leg of this table of your life, is what you accomplish. So many of us come from a broken past, broken homes or environments that were simply not conducive for learning some foundational principles of self-confidence, self-discipline or any number of essential, strategic mindsets for becoming successful. Many of us were allowed to just run wild and do whatever we want without any direction in life. The twenties pass, then the thirties and one day, we wake up in our forties and realize that we've accomplished very little. I think it's essential that young men in their late teens or early twenties are already asking themselves the hard question of who do they want to be? What do they want to accomplish and how do they intend to get there? A good father would be having this type of enlightening, maybe slightly confrontational yet essential conversation with their son or daughter in order to promote some thoughtful introspection on what one needs to start prioritizing and pursuing.

College isn't for everyone; I understand that. Maybe you've come to terms with the idea that college isn't your best move. You'd be pleased to know that in a recent study conducted by Entrepreneur.com of thirty millionaires, that over 20 percent of them had no secondary education. The path to success will certainly be blazed differently by each of us. If you have the hustle, the grit, the drive, and focused determination within you, then it truly doesn't matter what set of circumstances you were either born into or grew up with. It's never about what you were born into, but rather the drive you have in you to become more. You can go out and excel at any profession and do well for yourself. You can start at the bottom in any business and learn your trade, develop your craft and become a highly paid expert in any field. I see that exact scenario every day out here in the oilfields of North Dakota. Lots of people, both guys and gals, have come up here with nothing, getting here with little to no money, living in their cars in the Walmart parking lot, showering every other day at the truck stop, not knowing anyone or even the industry itself. Yet they quietly started to apply themselves, learning the work, building a resume of skills and over time have become both highly paid and highly sought after for their abilities and expertise. The question always boils down to whether you are willing to do whatever it takes to succeed. What challenges are before you that you must stare down and conquer in order to accomplish the life that you want for yourself and your loved ones?

As an example, when I started working up here in North Dakota, it required me to leave my wife and kids back in Colorado six weeks at a time before coming home for a week then doing it all over again. It was tough. I missed my people dearly. I missed birthdays and even my anniversary. I was exhausted all of the time, running a dirty log book while driving trucks. Many a night I spent sleeping up against the window in a day cab semi-truck parked at a production fluids disposal or a truck stop. I pulled many a thirty-six-hour-straight shift, sometimes back to back, with little sleep in between. It certainly wasn't the safest way to run, nor was it the most "legal." Yet, that's what it took to float the bills and get my wife through college. She now has a bachelor's degree in education. Some would say that I abandoned my wife for a year, leaving her the difficult responsibility of managing our children and our home all by herself. Others would commend me for working a year's worth of grueling hours, making $136,000 that year to invest the money and the time to see my family reunited in a better overall position a year later. My wife now makes a sizable income teaching at a Christian private school. I've dialed my work schedule back to four days a week. We enjoy kayaking at Spring Lake Park, having friends over for evening meals and now I get the money and the time. I just bought a lifted pickup truck, the truck that I've always wanted to have and it won't destroy me financially trying to make the payments. Aside from the enjoyment of what the investment now brings in monetary things, the real crowning jewel in all this is that my wife is now set up to function at a higher level financially if she ever had to do it alone. Remember this, the road to massive accomplishment and wild success is open to all. There is no discrimination in place preventing you or anyone else from achieving the life of your dreams.

I believe as men, it's in our genetics, in our very DNA, to be conquerors, to achieve greatness. I believe there's a purposeful overload of limiting distractions that exist in our world today, especially in America. All around us exist these tailor-made diversions that set and keep people on a path of mediocrity. Little things like social media, video games, alcohol, drugs, porn, and binge-watching Netflix, just to name a few. These are the things that keep people stuck in a perpetual place of "go nowhere, do nothing, accomplish nothing, become nothing." Mediocre. Never achieving. Never doing the hard work, which it is by the way, of pressing through the permeable membrane of stagnation to build a name for themselves and build a legacy of accomplishments that will define them, in part, as a man. Listen, if it were easy, my friend, then everyone would do it. If it were simple, then everyone would be an accomplished success but it isn't easy. It isn't free. I believe a man needs to be focused, to know what he wants, to make a plan and stick by it even when the difficult seasons appear to be impossible. It's never impossible. As Ryan Stewman says, the force of average is always trying to keep you down. It's like gravity. It takes inertia and perpetual motion constantly to press back on this natural force to keep you from being pulled back down into the humdrum of inferiority. We must set our sights on growth and success. We must stay focused and be relentless in the pursuit of our dreams. Just like Vikings that would pick countries and go conquer them, we need to make a plan and stick to it. We must demand of ourselves more territory and acquire the desires of our heart. I believe it's a calling. I believe it's a requirement for men to achieve great things. One, it provides for you an excellent life to be accomplishment-driven. However, it also sets the example for the people who are growing up underneath you to not be lethargic, to not be lazy, but to be accomplishment-driven as well. It serves the world better when men systematically set goals, and carry out those goals to their conclusion. The level of self-confidence that it naturally creates inside of us is worth the energy spent to become extraordinary. What do you dream about for yourself in the quiet of the night? Building a seven-figure business? Getting a degree? Owning a ranch in the country? Do you wish to create for yourself passive streams of income through real estate? Selling books or becoming the next YouTube sensation? How about marrying the woman of your dreams and starting a family? No one is placing a blockade in front of your dreams. If you can dream it, it can become a reality.

The next aspect of legacy is who you become. This one strikes home with me the most. There was a time in my life when I had become so defeated and so toxic that even I wouldn't want to be around the man who I then was. There was a time in my life where I was so lacking in self-confidence, self-esteem and self-worth that I couldn't believe I would ever be a man worthy of respect and admiration. I was severely bound in addictions to destructive habits. I was relentless in my quest to self-sabotage. I was forever plagued with a brokenness mindset that kept me stuck in a cyclical place of unproductivity. It's not a good place to be. It hurts deep inside to be nothing. It hurts deep inside to know that you're living beneath your capability. It hurts deep inside to know that no one loves or respects you as a man because your character and behavior don't afford you anyone's love or respect. It can hurt so bad that the only reprieve in life seems to be the mind-altering substances that you pump into your veins as often as you can. For many, this appears to be the only relief that can take away the cold reality that you're a dead man walking.

Who we become in our character and in our integrity as a man is tremendously important. It requires us to be honest with ourselves and ask some very pointed questions. It requires us to be self-analytical, often. Not just once, but at reoccurring points on our journey through life. We must learn to stop, sit down, tune out all the noise and distraction and ask ourselves, "Who am I becoming as a man? Am I grounded? Am I an emotionally secure person? Do I function from a place of positivity and courage or do I function from a place of fear and self-doubt? What is my character? How are my manners? What is my worldview? How do I see others? How do others perceive me? How do I see life and most importantly, if things stay the same, who will I become as a man?"

The willingness to frequently ask ourselves these difficult questions is not only important for our own growth and development, but they are essential questions that must be asked to determine the level of presence that we're bringing to the table as men in any given area. It should be noted that on occasion, if we're brutally honest with ourselves, there may be times and seasons where we do not like what we see. In this circumstance, the mindset that will separate the men from the boys and grant the most determined of us to see the results that we want is to allow the factual data to embolden us to press on, instead of becoming discouraged to the point where we quit and take the easier path of lethargic mediocrity. There must exist within each of us a level of ferocity and dedicated conviction to get up time and time again in the face of every failure and every setback to boldly and courageously triumph over the ugliest parts of ourselves. Never forget this truth; there are two men living inside of you. They are both hellbent on controlling your day-to-day life. If the wrong man assumes the throne, he will no doubt execute the other man to ensure that his rule and reign will continue unchallenged indefinitely. If the worst of you gains this authority, not only will he destroy your life but he will seek to exert his dominion and influence into the lives of your posterity through your negative influence. This is how he ensures his own immortality because, whether we intend to or not, you and I are quietly influencing the people around us. I want my children to grow up and take their lives, what they acquire, what they accomplish, who they become, and who they influence to levels of success that are beyond my own.

I want to see the people around me succeed. I want to become the type of man with who other people can feel safe and secure. I want to be the kind of man that's authentic. One who tells it like it is. A solid man that can sit down with somebody and have an honest, straightforward conversation without feeling like I have to put on a facade. I want to be the kind of man that other people are comfortable around to the point where they choose to be transparent, open up, and share the intimate details of their life because they realize that the quality of person that I am as a man is genuine. I want to be known as a noble, reliable person of influence. I want to heal the world around me. I want to impact and affect the world around me in a positive way. There are not enough men like this in the world today and the world suffers because of it.

We have to be able to detect toxicity in our mindset, in our habits, in our behaviors, and in our thought patterns. We have to be willing to search out the tools for healing so that we can begin to change who we are into who we want to become. Who we know, deep down in the innermost recesses of our souls, we were made to become. Apex masculinity is not about domination and chauvinism. It's about protecting those you love and care for. It's about developing those that you love and care for in a positive way, but you and I can't do this if we're toxic. You and I can't help other people become the best versions of themselves if we're stuck in a place of negativity and toxicity as men. We need to figure out what's broken, get it fixed, ensure that it stays fixed and consistently strive to grow and mature as men.

Lastly, the final aspect of our legacy deals with who we influence. We've discussed it briefly already but let's delve a little deeper into the concept of influence. I suppose that

I should be grateful for the fact that there is a definitive revolution taking place in the world today in which droves of men are finally pushing past their egos to engage in this process of personal growth and development. For many, pride no longer hinders us from being brutally honest with the reality that somewhere along our journey, we acquired toxic mindsets that have hindered us from evolving into the men who we know that we should be. I suppose that I should be appreciative of the fact that there is a global stirring in motion that appears to be shifting the consciousness of men to not succumb to the idea that what we now are is what we will always be. We can change. The desire to mature as men has gained enough popularity within our culture to where one should no longer feel as though he has to guard his reputation by hiding the fact that he's completely clueless as to what true manhood should look like. Long gone are the days of treating other people like shit through selfish, chauvinistic domination because we're really hiding that fact that we're hurting inside from a complete lack of understanding on how in the hell we're supposed to be carrying ourselves as men. It's OK to admit that our fathers, for whatever reason, failed us. Chances are that their fathers failed them. We would do well to remember that as we decide on how much animosity we're going choke ourselves with as we hold their failures against them. It's OK to admit that our rebelliousness as an adolescent hindered our fathers from being able to teach us how to be a man. Either way, admitting our weaknesses and our ignorance in understanding what true masculinity is has now become socially acceptable as long as one is willing to seek out the knowledge and the tools to exact change. The generational curse stops now. With us. With you.

So as you and I begin to deal with ourselves and start the process of evolving into our Apex Man, will we take anyone with us? It saddens me to my core to know that many men will sincerely, with genuine enthusiasm, start developing quality character traits within themselves but because they feel as though they haven't completely "arrived," they'll put off taking the time to invest in their wives and children to see them grow into the better versions of themselves. Don't keep this bottled up inside of you and please don't feel as though you have to be a perfect man before you can start training your sons and daughters how to be better people. Each of us is different, with our own personalized set of character flaws. You might spend the rest of your natural life fighting some of those particular flaws. Don't wait for self-perfection to start molding and shaping your kids. It's OK for them to see you fail at the same time that you're training them not to fail. Don't allow imposter syndrome or the feeling of being a hypocrite because you're not a top-notch man to prevent you from taking the time to invest into them what they are going to need to be successful in life. Teach them to be honest or they will lie at any cost and for any gain. Teach them some self-respect or they'll walk with their heads down and let people walk all over them. Teach them some manners or they'll struggle to understand boundaries. Teach them to care about themselves and their belongings or they'll live like pigs without good hygiene or cleanliness. Teach them to be gracious toward other people because there will come a day when they themselves have an epic blowout in character and they will want people to afford them forgiveness and grace. Teach them to believe in themselves by creating opportunities for them to succeed and reaffirming your belief in their ability to succeed through your spoken words. Stop being so critical of every mistake that they make or they will give up trying. Seriously though, learn to direct your fatherly, masculine, positively affirming and encouraging voice across the canyons of their hearts. Even on their worst days, when it seems as though they're making one mistake after another, make sure they know that you believe in their ability to succeed. Teach them to respect authority or they will float from one employment termination to the next. Teach them to see and admit their faults so that they don't become those ugly people who blame everyone else for their troubles, being self-deceived. Self-deception is the hardest flaw to heal from because it blinds us from knowing that we're stuck there. Teach them some self-control or they'll consume whatever they want whenever they want, destroying their health. They'll fly off the handle and verbally, or worse, physically abuse people. They'll crawl in the sack with anyone on a whim and create some lifelong unintended outcomes for themselves that don't often work out the way one would hope. Train your boys to keep their sexual passions in check or they will add tremendous undesired pain to their lives. I speak from personal experience. I lost three children decades ago because my toxic, uncontrolled passions were not in check. I wasn't ready to be a father, but the natural course of natural law waits for no one. Someone else got to raise my kids while I was in prison. He wasn't an Apex Man.

If you and I don't become Apex Men and then realize that it is a requirement, not an option but a requirement, to positively impact and influence those around us to also become apex, then we will have failed to do the greatest work. We will have created an anomaly in the generational chain by healing ourselves, but we will not have effectively broken the generational curse. The work may seem overwhelming at times but it's not as daunting as one might assume it to be. It simply starts with a wholehearted commitment to burn the bridges of complacency, put one foot forward and never look back. The end result of creating an apex family is well worth any of the difficulties that one will experience on the path. Remember, you're not alone. Although at times you may feel that way, keep in mind that there is an entire community of men who are making it their lifelong ambition to raise up exceptionally first-class people. These are the heroes of our time. The difference makers. There is no greater way to leave your mark and create a remarkably distinguished legacy. The world needs you. Don't fail us.

ABOUT THE AUTHOR

Nick Chontos is the founder and host of Apex Masculinity podcast, public speaker in addiction recovery groups, prisons and churches across America. Success coach and author of self-help literature for men by night and hydrovac operator in the frozen tundra oilfields of North Dakota by day. Father of 6 and happily married 14 years to his lovely wife Jessica.

Former meth addict of 8 years and two time convict, he now seeks to reach into the lives of broken men to help them recover from childhood trauma, abuse and destructive addictions to drugs, alcohol and pornography.

www.apexmasculinity.com

Made in the USA
Coppell, TX
25 November 2022

86978481R00127